UP

to

GOD

MOSAICA PRESS

UP
to
GOD

DOWN-TO-EARTH THOUGHTS
ON ELEVATED LIVING

D'VORAH MILLER

Published by Mosaica Press, Inc.
www.mosaicapress.com
info@mosaicapress.com

Dedicated as a *refuah sheleimah* for

Sarah bat Devorah

and in loving memory of

Ezriel ben David

"This work is refreshingly written. It contains brief but pithy insights into life's most important issues, based on the weekly Torah readings. Highly recommended."

Rabbi Dr. Akiva Tatz, founder and director
of Jerusalem Medical Ethics Forum,
author, senior lecturer at JLE-London

"With this book, D'vorah Miller has shared a universe of creative insights that merge ordinary experiences with extraordinary Biblical stories, showing us yet again how ancient wisdom still speaks so loudly to us today."

Dr. Erica Brown, author, lecturer,
and director of the Mayberg Center
for Jewish Education and Leadership

"I love it! D'vorah writes thought-provoking ideas about normal life. Let's be Normal. That's elevated living."

Rebbetzin Joanne Dove, senior educator,
SEED Adult and Family Jewish Education-UK

"My *talmidah* D'vorah Miller is well-known as an inspiring educator. This collection of writings demonstrates her ability to select fascinating material that makes a lasting impact upon our young people. It is my pleasure to recommend her book to all those attempting to maintain enthusiasm in their service of the Almighty."

Rabbi Dovid Refson, founder and dean
of Neve Yerushalayim College for Women

"D'vorah Miller has a unique way of distilling profound concepts in an easy-to-read, meaningful, and engaging style. D'vorah is a teacher's teacher. This book is filled with inspiration and insight into the ageless messages of our 4,000-year-old heritage."

Rabbi Dr. Ivan Lerner, industrial psychologist and lecturer,
Rabbi Emeritus of Claremont Wynberg Congregation, SA

Table of Contents

SHEMOT

VAYIKRA

BAMIDBAR

DEVARIM

FESTIVALS

Pre–Ramble

When I visit a particular website, I'm offered a choice:

"Yes, I want wisdom in my day."

"No, I'm happy without wisdom."

If I don't want to subscribe for notifications, I need to click:

"No, I'm happy without wisdom."

I'm a little defensive and also laughing as I click that choice, because I'm thinking, *You're backing me into a corner—I need to lie in order to find inspiration on your website without getting inundated.*

Of course I want wisdom. I just don't want more complexity to manage in my inbox. They don't offer that choice, though. There's nothing to click that says: "I love what your organization is offering, and I want wisdom every day, but I'm not subscribing, because I have a full life and I choose to be the daily decider of what will fuel me, and I don't find it helpful to be inundated with e-mails telling me what I'm missing or will be missing if I don't drop everything and tune in *now!*"

Yeah.

If you got this far, you're probably planning to read this book. If you decide not to read this book, I wouldn't assume that you don't want wisdom. Opportunities abound to increase wisdom. Having said that, I do hope you will find yourself wiser for this reading without unnecessary complexity to manage.

Thank you for choosing to read this book. If I already know you, I know that I'm grateful to you, for I cannot think of any person I know for whom I have no gratitude. And if I don't know you yet, I look forward to knowing you, and when we meet each other, please remind me I wrote that.

Acknowledgments

I am overwhelmingly grateful to the Source of all, with a depth that no expression can truthfully portray, for the mind and ideas to organize these writings in some coherent, valuable way; for the discipline to actually get it done; and for the courage to decide to be done, though nothing is ever done, just stopped.

Thanking people is risky—as is every valuable venture. It is also presumptuous to think that my appreciation could ever do justice to how much I am a beneficiary of the goodness of each of these people and all the people who won't even be mentioned here, plus all the authors, editors, and publishers of all the books and articles I've read, and the creators and contributors to circumstances I've experienced.

Thank you, Doron Kornbluth of Mosaica Press, for offering in 2013 to publish my writings after reading just a few of my articles. Your offer has been my glimmer of hope through busy and challenging circumstances, and it has continuously circled back to my consciousness at the times I thought my writings would never become a book, which was pretty much every other day. Thank you to Rayzel Broyde, art director; Sherie Gross, managing editor; Meira Lawrence, copyeditor; Daliya Shapiro, proofreader; and the rest of the staff at Mosaica Press for making this book a beautiful reality.

First, my parents: Ema and Abba—nothing I can say or write will ever suffice to thank you each and both for being people who are extraordinary heroes to so many and to me. Your joint choice to have a Torah home and to be an address for Jews searching for meaning became an invitation to your children to do the same. What I know about how to live, I've learned from you.

My in-laws: Mom—you are a gift of a mother-in-law, ever complimentary, ever encouraging, loving, and cheerleading. Since I first met you and Dad, I have only felt your complete embrace for your son's choice of me as his wife. May these writings bring you much comfort in this year of mourning Dad's passing, and may they facilitate an *aliyah* for the soul of Chaim Leib Yitzchak ben Moshe.

My awesome brothers and your holy wives: Doniel and Alyson, Ari and Shoshana, Ezra and Devoiry, and Michoel and Tamar, and your respective children and grandchildren—I love that we dream of spending time together. May Hashem shower you with daily revealed blessings.

To friends from childhood and various places I have lived: I am so much richer for your friendship.

I am appreciative to the individuals who influenced the following organizations and communities during the time I benefited from them: TA preschool—Baltimore; Hillel Academy—Pittsburgh; Hebrew Academy Lubavitch; Gan Yisrael and Long Beach Shul; Valley Torah High School; Bnot Chayil College; Neve Yerushalayim; West Coast NCSY; Telz Stone-Neve Tzion; Kenton Shul, Jewish Experience for Teens—London; MST College; Netzach Yisrael; New England NCSY; Boston Jewish community; Torah Academy; New England Hebrew Academy; Camp Dina; Ohr Somayach—Cape Town, South Africa; Phyllis Jowell Day School; Cape Town Torah High; Etz Chayim/JWRP—Baltimore; Ohr Chadash Academy; Irvine Hebrew Day School; Beth Jacob Irvine; the Jewish Collaborative of Orange County.

Our children: Yosef Aryeh, Akiva Yisrael, Hillel Shalom, Tehilah, Shoshanah, Betzalel, Miryam, Chavivah—I am grateful for the way that parenting each of you has challenged me to confront, discover, and create different aspects of my being. Pride is such an unsubstantial word to express the depth of my admiration for the fact that you all chart the course of your lives with faith, effort, humility, and humor. I daven deeply for your and your spouses' and children's continued health in all areas.

Our children-in-law: Gahi, Sara Tova, Yehudis, Natanel, Shlomo Zalman—Thank you, thank you for being the chosen life partners of our children and the dedicated parents of our grandchildren. I love you each and all.

Our grandchildren: I daven that you will reach for *simchah* and be open to seeing meaning in the struggles you will inevitably face as you grow into the *menschlich* people you will become.

My husband: We have not just been married to each other many years, we have been married to each other many times. I might easily have become all mother, yet you would not let me forget that I am my own woman and your wife. I am sometimes amazed at our bravery to venture (stumble) through discomfort toward honesty, so that we keep growing ourselves as individually accountable for our choices and we keep growing our relationship. I love that my adventure of life is with you. Also, on a practical note regarding this book—you have been my consistent cheerleader throughout the starts and stops of these writings. You have been telling me for years that you're so excited for my book to be published. Your confidence in me is majorly motivating. I think you were more distraught than I was when we thought all my writings were lost, when I spilled coffee on my laptop (and I hadn't properly saved everything—eek!). This book is yours too. So...yes, you can offer autographs at the book signings!

Introduction

The approach I take to Torah learning, teaching, and living is Mesoraic. It is a traditional, observant approach based on the idea that Torah is God-given, and Torah teachings have been passed through the generations from teachers to students, parents to children.

Hanging in our kitchen (with the knock-off brand of Scotch tape), there is a printout of a teacher-to-student line of Torah transmission from Moshe at Mount Sinai to today. The research was done by Rabbi Leib Kelemen.

The last name on the chain is Rabbi Henoch Lebowitz in 2008. My husband has added three more names to get us to my husband, whose rabbi was Dayan Gershon Lopian, zt"l.

While we don't presume that we are sages of the same stature listed on the chain, we want to remember that we value our connection to *mesorah*, the tradition tracing back to Sinai that provides a valid line for understanding halachah (Torah law). And we take our role in the chain of Jewish tradition seriously. We want our children to be connected to learning and the guidance from those who can trace their articulation of Torah to sources that have stood the test of time. Innovation and creativity are necessary for dynamic living, yet timeless principles must be recognized and respected if our innovations and creations are to last in a healthy way.

Years ago, I would begin my informal Torah classes with the stipulation that I was starting from a place of belief in the One absolute Creator, Sustainer, and Maintainer of the universe, Who provides Torah for us to connect to Him and to live our lives in the best way possible.

I did not have a formulaic way of presenting details of that stipulation. I simply wanted people to know that while "Where's God?" is a valid question, our learning of the day would not address that question. We were going to learn Torah from a place on the map that said: "God is here and this is His Torah."

Then, in Cape Town, South Africa, on a beautiful (southern hemisphere) fall day in 2015, in a conversation regarding curriculum for a Torah high school, Rebbetzin Zeesy Deren handed me a document that she had inherited. This was the treasure I did not even realize I had been searching for. It was a list of prerequisites and constant thoughts to keep in mind while studying Torah as an observant Jew. I was ecstatic; my heart was literally soaring! This was what I had been fumbling to articulate to anyone who wanted to appreciate the necessity and bliss and depth of the Torah learning experience.

Since that day, this list (with a bit of editing) has become the one to which I apply the motto: "Don't learn or teach Torah without it." Thank you, Zeesy.

I hope you, the reader, will find it a helpful window into the place from which I mindfully strive to learn and live, so that which flows from me may be a reflection of that striving.

Imperative Understanding:
Preparation and Intent for Learning Torah

1. Learning Torah is an opportunity to connect with Hashem.
2. Hashem is eternal and unchanging.
3. Hashem is absolute truth.
4. Torah is written concisely, with every detail and juxtaposition of events and narratives having untold and sacred significance.
5. Torah is Hashem's infinite wisdom and can never be fully understood; at the same time, it also allows for multiple levels of understanding.
6. The Written Torah and Oral Torah are one whole; they are fully dependent on one another.

7. Hashem gave us the rules and tools for learning Torah; these are also part of Torah.
8. Hashem transmitted His whole Torah to us through Moshe at Mount Sinai.
9. As a blueprint of creation, Torah is relevant in all areas of life, and everything is contained in it.
10. Torah is Hashem communicating to humans, guiding our lives, and teaching us lessons. It is not primarily a history book.
11. When applying Torah to our personal lives, we should use the guidance of other Torah sources to be sure we are taking a lesson that is in the spirit of what the Torah intends.
12. What happened to our forebears is a sign of what will happen to the Jewish People in the future, and gives us strength to endure similar challenges.

Since being introduced to this list of understandings, my husband and I have printed it and referred to it regularly by way of introduction to Torah study with both school students and adults. My husband has even assigned his high school students the task of memorizing it.

As I address students and adults from across the spectrum of beliefs and observance, I want people to know the place from which I approach my teaching. We will wrestle with wording in texts, question relevance, and struggle with application, because those are integral and necessary components of real, rigorous, thought-provoking, and soul-stirring learning. At the same time, know that I am wrestling, questioning, and struggling *inside* those twelve principles.

It's like being in a committed, loving relationship: I'll sometimes confront and question my spouse or my children and aspects of our relationships. If you don't know my broader commitment to certain principles/rules of our relationship, you (and I) may not understand that the ultimate purpose of my questioning and confronting is to strengthen our bonds of connection, so that I become a better person and we become a better pair focused toward a broader, greater good.

To Know before Reading

In writing, as in speaking, I often refer to God as "Hashem" (The Name).

For consistency's sake, I have chosen to use the Sephardic pronunciation for transliterated words.

I also prefer, where possible, to use the Hebrew pronunciations of names of Biblical personalities; the English pronunciations are readily available, so I like the idea of offering a learning opportunity to know the Hebrew names.

I refer to the Bible as the Torah because Torah means "teaching," "showing," and "instruction," which represent the purpose of Torah's existence.

Additionally, for smoother reading, and because I do not for a moment think that Hashem is limited by physical attributes, I consistently refer to God with the pronouns Him and He, although, throughout classical Jewish texts and liturgy, Hashem is referred to in alternating masculine/feminine forms depending on the ways in which we humans are experiencing Godly interactions.

> *By sharing my writings with the broader public, there are*
> *risks that bring me much discomfort:*
>
> *I become open to criticism to which I might not get an*
> *opportunity to respond.*
>
> *I can be wrong without the opportunity to self-correct.*
>
> *I can be misunderstood without the chance to clarify.*
>
> *With all that, with trepidation and love, I offer...*
>
> *Up to God*
>
> *Down-to-earth thoughts on living as a Jew.*

What's It For?

We can only use what we have. We can only do the best we can with what we know. When we hold a tool in our hands without knowing what it can do, its power will be lost on us. If we don't ever learn its purpose, and if we don't ever learn how to use it, we'll just carry the tool until it gets too heavy to lug around. The more we know about the purpose of the tool and the rules for reaching that purpose, the more we will be free to move toward that purpose.

This goes for everything, the broadest of which is life itself. The situation of life is a tool. It is an instrument packed with potential to move closer to God, and that is the purpose of the tool.

We cannot choose a way to get close to Him other than through living the way He wants us to live. Yet we will never master all the myriad details of how to reach that ultimate level of closeness—the ultimate freedom from worldly constraints. My husband is fond of saying that he is not free on the guitar. Many will vouch for his great guitar playing, me included. He plays some pretty good stuff. Yet he thinks, *If only I had more lessons and more practice, I'd know more, and when I play, I'd play so much better.*

He knows the guitar is a tool for music. He even knows how to use it. Still, he sometimes feels frustrated knowing there's so much more potential to be tapped, and he will never fully master the guitar. Does this mean he should not even attempt some level of mastery? If the ultimate goal is unattainable, is the effort futile?

Is it like asking if we should not attempt any pursuit of intellectual understanding because we will never possess all the knowledge in the world? Or how about this one: We will never live forever, hence should we simply neglect our health? (Answer to both questions: Nay! Lest we expire dumb and young.)

We know the correct response. We know that our efforts toward growth are valuable. It's just that sometimes we get lost. Sometimes we forget that life is a tool to utilize in ways that move us toward God. When we feel frustrated that we have not mastered the tool of life, life itself can feel burdensome. That's a really good time to remember we are human, for God's sake!

If we are dragging life around rather than using it to unlock goodness in each moment, we can stop lugging! We can know that the instrument of life is meant to be played purposefully. Then its power will be found in us. And even though we will never completely master the instrument—we can play some pretty good stuff.

Stop in the Name of God

SHABBAT

Practice does not make perfect. Still, practice gets us a whole lot further than no practice. If an individual never practices ceasing, he or she will barely know how to cease.

Shabbat is a day of ceasing. During the week, we work toward what can be. We do creative work, which in Hebrew is called *melachah*. There is an immeasurable amount of *melachah* to be done in this world, and just the thought of that truth can exhaust us.

So what can fuel us to be continuously involved in *melachah* throughout the week? I want to suggest that an underlying hum of Shabbat—a constant knowledge that I would still have worth even if I were to cease plotting, planning, and creating—can fuel us. The notion that I only have worth because I work may motivate me for a while, but it will eventually leave me exhausted—thinking I will never be enough, no matter what I do and accomplish.

The Chafetz Chaim, Rabbi Yisrael Meir Kagan (Poland, 1838–1933), said that while we won back Shabbat in America—because by the 1930s, Jews could make a decent living and still keep Shabbat—we had lost Erev Shabbat. We had lost the art of proper preparation for the day of ceasing.

> The notion that I only have worth because I work may motivate me for a while, but it will eventually leave me exhausted—thinking I will never be enough, no matter what I do and accomplish.

How do we prepare for Shabbat? I'm not referring to making matzah balls and schnitzel. I'm referring to preparing ourselves to be receivers of the Shabbat Queen: preparing our minds, bodies, and souls. I believe we need daily Shabbat drills—daily times when we practice speech and behaviors of ceasing, so that when we reach Shabbat, we'll be prepared to more wholly cease.

Here are four thoughts that can translate into "stops," which can then become daily habits.

1. I can stop and celebrate even when circumstances and people are not perfect. When I learn with brides about *taharat ha'mishpachah*, Jewish marriage laws, I talk about the relationship-building exercise of regularly suspending expectations; to move from disconnection to acceptance, embrace, and, ultimately, celebration of your spouse. The monthly reunion between husband and wife is the perfect reminder that amid imperfection, we can stop and enjoy time together.

2. I can stop and make realistic plans with time for breaks and interruptions. When one of our daughters had a full day of exams in school, she found herself standing and stretching after the first two hours of focused work. Knowing that most of her classmates had some type of medication to help them focus and/or feel calmer throughout the day, it came as no surprise to her when the teacher, who was proctoring the exams, suggested that our daughter might want to look into taking medication herself. Our daughter, without skipping a beat, in her frank way, looked the

teacher in the eye and stated emphatically: "I don't need drugs. I just need a break." When we value our mental, emotional, social, and spiritual health, when we care enough about bringing our whole selves to our interactions, we'll set boundaries in time for regrouping, refreshing, processing, assessing, noticing, embracing, and "gratitude-ing."

3. I can stop and talk to Hashem from where I am without waiting to feel worthy. A parent who loves his child knows the value of a phone call from a child when that child is in trouble. While God wants us to be in healthy spaces, He also wants us to reach out when we're not.

4. When I feel joy, I can stop and thank Hashem directly, focusing on gratitude, not worry. Professor Brené Brown has researched what brings people to live wholeheartedly. She found that some people, in moments of joy, start to worry about all the things that could go wrong. This worry caps their joy. Others—those who live wholeheartedly—shift away from worry and into gratitude in moments of joy. "*Modeh ani*—Thankful am I [to You, Hashem]" is a phrase worth articulating, not just upon arising, but to keep us from slipping into worry at the twists and turns of each day.

In *Megillat Eichah* there is a verse that is understood as referring to our response to the destruction of Jerusalem.[1] The verse is commonly translated as, "Gone is joy of our hearts; turned into mourning is our dancing." The word for "gone" here in Hebrew is *shavat*, and the word for "our dancing" is *mecholeinu*, which can also be translated as "from our weekday (*chol*)."

Rabbi Mendel of Rimanov understands the passage as follows: "Shabbat—the joy in our hearts—has turned into mourning from [the way we spend] our weekday." In other words, the way we spend our weekdays is intrinsically linked to our Shabbat experience. Shabbat is a twenty-five-hour suspension of expectations, a wholehearted

---

1   5:15.

acceptance, embrace, and celebration of what *is*. It is the day that we stop striving and just be. Not because we have completed our work; just because it's time to stop, to pause.

The artist is never finished; he just stops. We are each the artist of our lives. And it benefits us to know how to stop. If we are to come to a full stop and remain there for twenty-five hours every week, we need to have some practice during the week. When we have daily access to the power of ceasing, we can know how to plug into Shabbat.

I am suggesting that we practice these four "stops" every day:

1. Stop in order to celebrate.
2. Stop in order to refresh.
3. Stop in order to speak to Hashem.
4. Stop in order to feel gratitude instead of worry.

There is an idea that as we buy and prepare food and other items for Shabbat, we should say, "*Lichvod Shabbat*—In honor of Shabbat." These words raise our awareness of the purpose of those activities. In a similar vein, as we practice each of these stops, we can say, "*Lichvod Shabbat*—In honor of ceasing." In this way, we tap into a hum of acceptance, embrace, and celebration during the week.

Then, though we still may not always land comfortably into the territory of the weekly Shabbat, at least that ceasing space won't feel completely foreign.

And though that's not perfect, it's a whole lot further than we'd be without the practice.

And that's enough for now.

BEREISHIT

Husbands and Wives for Good

BEREISHIT

God gave the first man a partner.

Not a silent one.

Not a buddy.

A woman.

God refers to her as *"Ezer k'negdo." Ezer* means "help," while *k'negdo* is *neged*, meaning "facing" or "opposite"—as in "The Jews encamped *neged* Har Sinai."[1]

So woman was created as a helper facing/opposite him. From that vantage point, she can see his goodness and his faults, and she can both complement and confront him. That idea is enough to get us started on the road to understanding why Hashem calls Chavah *"k'negdo."*

---

1   *Devarim* 19:2.

Still, there's more. *K'negdo* is an interesting expression. It can also mean "having to do with," as in "*k'neged*" the four sons in the Haggadah. With this understanding, *ezer k'negdo* would translate as "a helper having to do with him."

So woman is a "helper" with different roles. The thing is, the Torah doesn't say that Adam needed help. Nowhere do we find that he was sick and in need of a doctor, or that he was in trouble and needed a lawyer, or that he was wracked with anxiety and could use a good therapist.

A possible hint that help was necessary is when, just prior to the creation of woman, God says, "It is not good for man to be alone."[2] God uses the word *tov*, "good," to describe what was missing for man. When we say something is "good," we are saying that it works for us; it fits into our plans. When God says something is "good," it means that it is fulfilling its purpose by properly connecting to Him.

> When we say something is "good," we are saying that it works for us; it fits into our plans. When God says something is "good," it means that it is fulfilling its purpose by properly connecting to Him.

Therefore, "It is not 'good' for man to be alone" means "It is not a way to connect to God for man to be alone." And in this case, the opportunity for *tov*, goodness, comes in the form of an *ezer k'negdo*.

From this explanation, we can see the importance of the woman being strong in her personal connection to God. For she is to be a continual point of connection to God—not just for herself, but for her husband. The damsel in distress is as far from a Torah idea as you can get!

From our first explanation of *k'negdo*, I know that a wife is on the right track when she faces her husband with either acceptance or opposition, depending on what he needs. This is about her direct interactions with her husband.

And with *k'negdo* as "having to do with him," I get more insight: A wife's relationship with her husband is not just about face-to-face

---

2   *Bereishit* 2:18.

interactions, compliments, and criticism. She can be "a helper having to do with him" by preparing provisions, space, and an atmosphere that invites connection. Additionally, by providing opportunities for him to appreciate her, he can therefore feel close to God in all that he has been blessed with. A friend of mine once told me that she asks herself every afternoon, "What have I done for my husband?" This is not a meek woman stuck in a place she does not want to be. This is a woman who recognizes her worth and the power of her efforts to affect her husband while becoming her more actualized self.

Adam valued Chavah from the get-go. He knew God created him as lacking without her. He knew he was ultimately dependent on Hashem, Who wanted him to share his life with Chavah.

And from that get-go, Chavah knew her purpose. She knew she was being cared for by Hashem, Who wanted her to live up to the reason He created her as a separate being.

All was clear…until Chavah and Adam ate from the Tree of Knowledge of good and evil, and then, everything changed. Now there was not just truth and falsehood from which to choose; there was good and evil intertwined in each of them. Now they had new emotional and physical desires to sift through as they made their choices.

We live in this changed world. Here, husbands do not naturally value their wives, and wives underestimate the crucial role of *ezer k'negdo*. We live in a world that has us questioning the value of marriage altogether, and in which we find apparent confusion about the purpose of life and therefore confusion about what is truly valuable.

The purpose of life is to bind ourselves to God through the ways the Torah prescribes. The purpose of marriage is to bind ourselves to our spouses through the ways the Torah prescribes.

By being connected to Torah, we can have a level of clarity, "*k'neged*"—having to do with—the best picture of marriage. And it is Good, with a capital G—in the way God intends.

The Cover Story

NOACH

In the year 2000, when we were living in London, my husband had an office overlooking Edgware Road. One day, while working on a program in that office, I chanced to look out the window and saw that a new advertisement for toilet paper had been freshly posted on the billboard across the street. I was mortified by the blatant disregard for basic standards of modesty. Appalled, I quickly closed the shades and moved on with my work. All day, though, I found myself bothered by the thought that hundreds of people driving down the road would have to see that ad, without a choice in the matter.

Still agitated that evening, I decided to take action. After the kids were sleeping, I took the keys to my husband's office and asked if he would mind if I went out for an hour. In the office, I procured a large roll of colored paper, thick black markers, and lots of sticky tape. I worked on the massive poster for about forty minutes. Then I put it in my car and drove across the street. I parked my car just under the advertisement. I climbed onto the roof of my car, holding my poster. I stretched it as far across the billboard as I could, covering the offending picture.

I stuck it up with a whole roll of sticky tape. I stepped back (without falling off the roof of my car), satisfied. The words "SUPPORT HUMAN DIGNITY" now shouted out over the undignified advertisement. That was my little social justice project of the night.

Soon after the Great Flood, Cham, father of Canaan, went into his father's tent and saw his sleeping father, Noach, drunk and unclothed. Unabashed, he went outside to inform his brothers about the state of their father. The brothers, Shem and Yefet, responded by entering their father's room to cover him.

Here's Noach's response when he sobers up: "Cursed is Canaan! He shall be a slave to his brothers."[1]

And then, "Blessed be God, the Lord of Shem! Canaan shall be his slave. May God make Yefet beautiful, and he will dwell in the tents of Shem, and Canaan will be their slave."[2]

While commentators discuss what Cham actually did to his father that made him deserving of such curses, Rabbi Shimshon Raphael Hirsch discusses the improper attitude of a man, who was already a father himself, to violate his father's privacy.

So here's my question: If Shem and Yefet wanted to show that they truly respected their father Noach's privacy, why did they enter the room at all? "Look, we don't go into Dad's room. If he's uncovered in his own room, it's his business, not ours. We respect his privacy!"

That is a high level of respect.

However, there is a greater level still.

In July 1993, we were living in Israel, and I was seven months' pregnant with our third child. One night, in the week before Tishah B'Av, my husband and I rushed to Bikur Cholim hospital, as I was in excruciating pain. Once the practitioners assessed that it was not a kidney stone, which I had suffered from in the past, my pain was diagnosed as resulting from a large ovarian cyst.

---

1   *Bereishit* 9:25.
2   Ibid., 9:26.

Thank God, after much madness, the cyst was successfully removed by a competent surgeon, and I healed sufficiently to give birth to Hillel Shalom, *b'shaah tovah*, at full term.

How does this relate to Noach?

Regarding Cham's brothers, the Torah tells us: "Shem and Yefet took the garment and placed it upon both their shoulders and, walking backward, covered their father's nakedness..."[3]

When I was lying on that operating table, I was wide awake (my pregnancy vetoed the option of general anesthesia, and I was given an epidural). Besides the strangeness of the sensations of being operated on, I experienced a deep sense of exposure. Curious faces peeked in through observation windows, as this particular surgery was a learning opportunity for doctoral students. The expense of their learning opportunity was my extreme vulnerability. I remember feeling an overwhelming desire to cover myself. The desire was all consuming; it was deeply painful.

When the surgery had been successfully completed, and I was still on the operating table, my thoughts were only, *I need to be covered.*

Then came a comfort so profound. One man, wearing a *kippah*, perhaps a doctor-in-training, simply placed a sheet over me, up to my neck. Then he left. My gratitude was immense. My honor had been protected. So powerful was this experience that I couldn't speak of it for years.

That man could have simply exited the operating room like everyone else once the surgery was complete. But he chose to behave altogether differently; he actively restored my sense of dignity. I could not imagine ever being able to repay his kindness. I did go back to the hospital a few months later, looking to thank him, but I never could find out who he was.

When Shem and Yefet stood outside, they were respecting their father's privacy. Had they remained outside after Cham trampled on that privacy, they would have been seen as respectful.

---

3   Ibid., 9:23.

Yet the circumstances invited a higher level of respect. Noach's privacy had been invaded. Therein lay the opportunity for the restoration of his dignity, and that is the opportunity the brothers seized. From their action, Noach saw reason to bless Hashem. As shame was concealed, *kiddush Hashem*, sanctification of Godliness, was revealed.

In our everyday lives, we can look for and act upon chances to restore human dignity.

I'm not referring to making posters (or standing on cars in the dark). I mean being particular to respect the privacy of others, and not to expose their vulnerabilities.

Not to tear down their defenses. And further, to give cover when appropriate.

Intentions Aside

NOACH

When I awoke, I detected a strange odor. Then I heard a thud and some scrambling. Little-boy feet. Two pairs, belonging to our two-year-old and three-year-old, respectively. In my sleepy brain, I debated going back to sleep. A few lines of dawn's early light lazily peeked through the slats in the Israeli *tris* (blackout blinds).

I could close my eyes and pretend I didn't know there was going to be some necessary intervention and probably a major mess and maybe even bodily injury to contend with when I ventured out into the big wide world of my children's escapades.

As I did not yet hear any cries or screams, it was safe to presume the two mischief-makers were in cahoots thus far. As much as I knew that could mean active destruction of property, I found some comfort in the idea of the boys working together rather than against each other.

When I had imagined sufficient damage to get myself out of bed and silently crack open the bedroom door enough to get a glimpse of the hallway, a sense of defeat swept through my still-so-tired brain before

I could decide on a way forward. The urge to climb back into bed and let their father deal with it upon his awakening was strong.

I mustered courage from some unexplainable mommy place and set forth to survey the scene. Raw, frozen chickens were lined up on the floor, making a line from the kitchen, through the living room, down the hallway, past the bathroom, and into the boys' bedroom. There was a foot or so between each frozen bird. The spacing appeared to be intentional.

As we had, just the day before, lugged in a huge order of frozen chickens for the upcoming holidays, I knew this activity could continue for a while.

I could hear the boys in the kitchen, and they hadn't seen me yet, so I headed for their bedroom. The line stretched along the floor, across the porch off their bedroom, to the last chicken perched atop the porch wall as if ready for take-off. I peered over the wall to see two already-launched chickens, which had apparently recently plunged to their demise. Frozen chickens are heavy! The thought of someone being hit on the head by a falling frozen chicken motivated me to remove the ready-for-takeoff chicken atop the wall and head for the kitchen to put a halt to this poultry activity.

In the kitchen, I found the three-year-old standing on a chair with his head in the freezer, pulling out the next frozen chicken to hand down to the two-year-old, who seemed to be the liner-upper of the birds. The boys seemed immune to what looked like frostbite on their little hands, so involved were they in carrying out this project. I experienced a subtle admiration for their determination, as I also realized that the boys probably would not have been able to carry out this project had they not joined forces.

Needless to say, I was the killjoy who put a stop to the joint efforts of the two rascals who had hatched this plan that no doubt had some intention behind it.

Perhaps later there would be space for discussions on poultry transport and the fine line between genius and weirdness. But for now, whatever the intentions, I didn't want them dragging raw chickens across floors and catapulting them onto unsuspecting pedestrians.

Then, I set them up with activities in separate rooms so I could get to the work of cleaning up without them immediately pursuing the next potentially harmful venture.

In *Parashat Noach*, we meet the builders of the Tower of Bavel.

In examining those builders, our Sages are interested in their intentions.

Why were the people building a tower?

- To fight God (Gemara, *Sanhedrin*)
- To make themselves into gods (*Ramban*)
- To seat King Nimrod on the highest throne to supervise the world (*Seforno*)
- To create a guarding idol as protection from natural disasters (*Haketav V'Hakabbalah*)
- To keep all mankind concentrated in one place (*Rabbeinu Bachya, Kli Yakar, Ohr Hachaim*)
- To surround Avraham and keep him from spreading the idea of one God to all the nations (Rabbi Yosef Tzvi Dushinsky)

All agree on what was done. All differ on why. And all can be simultaneously correct.

Numerous are the intentions of one act, in one mind. How much more so in the minds of many.

The *Sefat Emet*, Rabbi Yehuda Leib Alter of Ger, presents a fascinating insight into the Tower of Bavel builders, also known as the *Dor Haflagah*, "Generation of the Separation." His explanation sheds light on why that generation was not wiped out like the *Dor Hamabul*, "Generation of the Flood."

The *Dor Hamabul* lived by base instinct. Their behavior reflected pure animalistic drives and nothing more. They took whatever they felt like taking, and they satiated immediate desires with nary a thought of consequence. We must know that in such conditions, civilization will not endure. In this case, the result was the frightening erasure of all humanity except for the eight members of Noach's family.

The behavior of the *Dor Haflagah*, on the other hand, was different. Whatever their myriad intentions, the builders used their minds intelligently. Their actions showed motivation beyond satiating personal desires. There was some higher-level thinking or feeling involved, some intellectual or spiritual content at work. While the people in the generation of the flood behaved like animals, the people building the tower behaved like humans.

When Avraham hit the scene, God would expect a core of "above-human" behavior. The seeds of the Jewish nation would need to behave in a Godly manner.

In the meantime, the basis for all civilization was being considered. It needed to contain levels of intelligence and spirituality, and it did, which is why the people were not destroyed; they were merely separated by language barriers.

Separating joint task forces is sometimes called for, especially when it is in their unity that more harm than good seems likely to follow.

Because sometimes, whatever the intentions, the chicken catapulting must stop.

A Separate Piece

NOACH

"Rebbetzin, the challah is sick!"

We were living in Israel in the early '90s, and five teenage yeshiva students sat around our little Shabbat table.

"Sick?" I questioned. They assured me that it was a compliment.

What is it we are doing when we separate challah? We are giving up a portion of what we call "ours," and then we can enjoy the rest. Bread baked from a large batch of dough without challah taken is unfit for a Jew to eat. Once we separate that piece of "our" dough, the rest of the dough becomes permissible to us and can serve a purpose.

This week we celebrate Shabbat within the South African Chief Rabbi's vision of the Shabbat Project. Shabbat is the day we separate from the rest of the week. We offer Hashem the day of Shabbat. If our week was dough, Shabbat would be the piece we are *mafrish* (separate). It is a chunk of "our" time that we take out.

As with challah, it is the keeping of Shabbat—as separate—that allows the mundane rest of the week to be utilized purposefully.

Whenever my husband and I have attended any of our children's siddur plays, we've watched the children display an untainted, sweet eagerness for connection to prayer. I am moved to tears by the simple and pure separateness of a child's excitement against the backdrop of the knowledge that the reality of the mundane will in time threaten to overtake that pure separateness.

I realize that by holding those moments of pure separation from mundane, the mundane becomes purposeful. The Hebrew word *challah* is derived from the word *chol*, "mundane." The piece we separate is itself mundane. Yet by setting aside a portion, by giving in the way Hashem prescribes, we render the rest of the dough suitable—purposeful.[1]

We met the Generation of the Flood in *Parashat Noach*. Don't get too comfortable with that lot, though, because they meet their demise soon after we learn they were corrupt. What did they do wrong? They stole. They already had everything they could possibly need and use, yet they took from each other. When a person takes, it's because he perceives that he's lacking. The people were lacking an understanding of their purpose. Each person thought that the purpose of life was his own pleasure. They separated nothing for each other, and they sanctified nothing to God. The world had become like a batch of dough without challah taken.

> When a person takes, it's because he perceives that he's lacking. The people were lacking an understanding of their purpose.

Potentially delectable, presently purposeless.

This week, we all offer Shabbat to Hashem, though it's already His, as is the whole week. Once we "give up" the seventh day by offering Shabbat in the prescribed manner, the rest of our week becomes purposeful. The opportunities to recognize God arise throughout the mundane week. We feel less lacking; we look not to take but to give. And that is healthy—not sick.

---

1   *Bamidbar* 15:19–11.

Avraham and the Shabbos Project

LECH LECHA

I want to know exactly why Avraham merited to have Hashem appear to him. The Torah doesn't tell me!

Earlier, the Torah states clearly: "Noach was a *tzaddik* (a righteous man)."

Yet regarding Avraham, the Torah gives no information regarding God's opinion of Avraham's spiritual status. Not only that, Avraham's whole past is mysterious. Our understanding of his childhood and early adulthood is based on midrash and Oral Tradition.

Why does Hashem leave such a gaping hole in His Written Torah when it comes to the early life of the father of monotheism and Judaism? I want to know what earned Avraham such merit.

The words of the *Maharal*, Rabbi Yehuda Loew of Prague (1520–1609), speak to me. (No, I am not hearing voices). The *Maharal* says that Hashem didn't give reason for Avraham's merit because we shouldn't think that we know why Hashem appeared to Avraham and made a covenant with him.

If we knew the details of Avraham's early life, we might come to assume that Hashem's covenant with Avraham regarding the Jewish People is dependent on a specific set of unique behaviors and circumstances. This could lead us to think that if we do not express those exact behaviors in those unique circumstances, we may be unworthy of being Hashem's representatives in this world.

In other words, we might think that Hashem will, so to speak, change His mind about choosing us to be the soul of the world. This is a damaging line of thought. Hashem does not want us to reach that false conclusion. Only Hashem knows His reasons for choosing Avraham, and His covenant with the Jewish People is for all time. The *Maharal* says that this is the true conclusion Hashem wants us to reach from learning about His relationship with Avraham Avinu.

Around the time of year of *Parashat Lech Lecha*, many communities celebrate "The Shabbos Project." Jews are encouraged to keep Shabbat; to refrain from the mundane.

"More than the Jew has kept Shabbat, Shabbat has kept the Jew." Shabbat is a sign we carry to show we are open for the business of being God's representatives.

The Chafetz Chaim gives a parable: When a store that is usually open closes for one day, people assume it's still in business. If the next day they see through the shop window the shopkeeper removing items from the shelves, people can still think the shop will reopen soon. But when, finally, the sign above the shop is taken down, it is clear the shop has closed down. Shabbat is the sign above the shop.

As long as we keep that sign, we are in business.

Keeping Shabbat is the fourth of the Ten Commandments, after "Do not take God's name in vain" and before "Honor your father and mother."

- Keeping Shabbat is what Avraham and Sarah did.
- Keeping Shabbat is what Yitzchak, Rivkah, Yaakov, Rachel, Leah, Levi, Amram, Yocheved, Moshe, Tzipporah, and every Jew who stood at Sinai did.

- Keeping Shabbat is what every Jew who has taken responsibility for Judaism has done since that year, 1312 BCE.
- In every generation, past, present, and future, there were, are, and will be individuals and communities living with the awareness of the privilege to nourish their own souls and the soul of the world—the Jewish nation—through observing Shabbat.
- Hashem made an eternal promise to Avraham that the Jewish nation would be everlasting.
- I choose to be a player in the fulfillment of that promise.

Have a wonderful Shabbat!

What's in It for Me?

LECH LECHA

"A scout helps at all times without expecting reward."
Betzalel Miller, quoting the Scout Handbook as he stacks
chairs to be helpful at an event (2011 CE)

*"Be like the servants who serve their master not in order
to receive a reward."*
Antigonus Ish Socho, quoting Shimon HaTzaddik
in Pirkei Avos (50 BCE)

The Scouts are on to something.

Avram (later Avraham) is told by Hashem to leave home and go to the place that He will show him. Our *mesorah* (tradition tracing back to Sinai) tells us that this is one of Avram's ten trials of faith.

We usually think of Avram's leaving everything familiar as so difficult for him, but right after Hashem tells Avram to go, He also tells Avram that he will be great and wealthy!

Wait a minute...If Avram knows that Hashem is going to make him great and wealthy after he leaves behind everything familiar, he has that reassurance to ease any anxiety that might accompany the move. If so, then what was the trial in following God's command here? And why did God give Avram that glimpse into the future if it was meant to be a test?

If I had crystal-ball clarity that all would be great after I did something difficult, I imagine I would have no qualms about tackling that task with confidence.

Let's back up: What is the purpose of offering a reward? A reward can be a motivational tool, to gain cooperation:

"After you clean your room, you can have ice cream."

What's the purpose here? To get the kid to clean his room. Is that the end, though? Does a parent just want a clean room? Well, maybe. But good parenting takes into account the ultimate goal here—to build a responsible human being.

And what does a responsible human being look like? That will vary, depending on how much you let God into your life. The Torah view is that our best selves are the selves most bound to God. From this perspective, a responsible human being is one who knows that being his best self is a continuous process of being in a relationship with God. With this awareness, the offering of reward should complement the growth of the relationship, until the strengthened relationship becomes the reward itself. Then, seeming rewards become not motivations of isolated pleasure but opportunities for further bonding.

> The Torah view is that our best selves are the selves most bound to God.

Back to Avram, if he was assured of fortune, what was the test? It seems Avram's test was all about...intention. Would Avram follow the command just to get to the material goods? Or would he follow Hashem's command for the opportunity to contribute to the relationship? The fortune and fame were going to follow, but would Avram see those as end goals or as opportunities to grow closer to the Source?

There's something I find fascinating in this idea. God could have just told Avram, "*Lech*—Go." Hashem didn't need to tell Avram that wealth would follow, because Avram would have gone regardless. After all, Avram already knew he was different from his family. He already sensed he had a different calling. By the time Hashem says "Go," Avram is ready to make that step. It's like a marriage proposal. In a real relationship, the couple knows they are at the point where marriage is the next step. It's not a matter of if; it's a matter of when.

If the test is about intention, my thought is that sometimes the purpose of offering rewards is an opportunity to gauge where I am on the spectrum of connection in a relationship. If I desire to continuously strengthen a relationship, then a promise of some future "reward" can simply be a promise of future opportunities for more relationship strengthening.

The promise of fortune and fame is the promise of the chance to use circumstances and material possessions in service of the relationship. In this light, the reward is not a lure—it is the next challenge.

So what does it mean to not desire reward? I believe it means not to desire reward simply for the immediate pleasure it will bring. Rather, embrace the reward, including the pleasure it brings as a means to deepening the relationship.

In other words, we can be in each moment, serving God not for what will come next, but for what is right now—a strengthened bond—an excellently tied knot. Which, incidentally, the Scouts are famous for.

A Peace of Difference

LECH LECHA

I imagine it was not difficult for Avram to break the news to Sarai that they were moving. After all, this was a command from Hashem Himself. And tradition has it that Sarai would teach women all about the one God, while Avram taught the men. There was probably not much discussion on the matter. This is not because the couple had the same way of thinking, though. As we learn more about the original Patriarch and Matriarch, we see that their personalities were very different from each other. Yet it seems they were able to function in that elusive state of marital harmony called *shalom bayit*.

When a husband and wife exercise discipline in appreciating their differences for the sake of the wholeness of the relationship, there is said to be *shalom bayit*, "peace in the home." Making peace is a creative endeavor. Peace is a state that we reveal through our speech, actions, and attitudes, and God gives us opportunities to pursue, make, and keep peace.

Contrary to popular belief, *shalom* (often translated as "peace") is not the absence of difference or disagreement. If it were, no real relationship would be *b'shalom*. Rather, *shalom* is when people can be "together"—united with respect despite their differences.

From the distinctive traits of our ancestors, we can reinforce this concept:

- Avraham was known for acts of kindness.
- Sarah had a clarity of justice.
- Yitzchak was the epitome of absolute acceptance of God's will.
- Rivkah was the embodiment of caring for the well-being of others.
- Yaakov represented Torah—the study and pursuit of fulfilling God's will.
- Rachel lived by selfless giving.
- Leah demonstrated the power of prayer to change oneself.

And it's not only in husband/wife relationships that peace can be revealed through differences.

- There are twelve tribes, each with their unique strengths and avenues to God.

And later…

- Moshe was an intellectually towering leader, while his brother, Aharon, was an expert in inspiring social and emotional connections.
- Miriam lived with a faithful vision, while her husband, Nachshon ben Aminadav, exemplified active courage.

Soon after…

- Calev was unswayed by the betrayal of the spies surrounding him, while Yehoshua feared being influenced by the people, yet it was his desire to understand the people that made him the next leader of choice.

So many personalities. And we are introduced to them all. This could be because we need to appreciate difference—to see it as Hashem's way of entrusting us with the decision to make or break peace. If absence of difference is the goal of life, it would be best to seek only the company of those most like you.

Then...

- Avraham should have had a wife like Rivkah.
- Sarah should have had a husband with the traits of her son, Yitzchak.
- There would be no need for twelve tribes; we could be one big tribe!
- Moshe and Aharon should have been one superman, as should have Calev and Yehoshua.

As much as we enjoy the comfort that comes with agreement, there is no dynamic in a relationship of total agreement, and no energy being expended in an effort to create *shalom*. *Shalom* stands when I can be different from you, and at the same time aim to love you with complete respect for your being. When I find my frustration rising at your inability to see the clarity of my reasoning, I need to remember that a differing opinion or tendency is an invitation to become more than I am now, thus uncovering Hashem in this world.

> *Shalom* stands when I can be different from you, and at the same time aim to love you with complete respect for your being.

Halachah (Jewish law) invites me to show *kavod ha'briot*, "respect for God's creations," but it does not require me to convince others that I am right. Even the commandment to rebuke my friend is only a commandment that pertains to me if three criteria are met first: I love my friend (meaning, I want what is best for him), I am certain his actions are harmful, and he is open to hearing me. In this way, the rebuke will not demean his dignity—or mine.

Daily, I have opportunities to define myself as being *b'shalom*. When I remember that people are purposefully created with different natures and different ways of thinking, which lead to different emotions and actions, I can decide to not be threatened by difference. On the contrary, I don't want to miss these moments to respect you; not just in spite of our differences, but because of them.

Best Laid Plains

VAYEIRA

It is sweltering hot.

Avraham is situated at the entrance of his home, yearning for the emergence of guests. It is three days after his circumcision, and God appears to Avraham in the "Plains of Mamre."

The name Mamre is familiar. We find in *Midrash Rabbah* that Avraham had three friends: Aner, Eshkol, and Mamre. Earlier, Avraham had asked for their advice regarding God's command of circumcision.

- Aner said, "You are old, it will be painful."
- Eshkol said, "Why make yourself look different than your enemies [giving them reason to hate you]?"
- Mamre said, "This is the same God who has protected you until now. You can trust Him."

What is this midrash telling us? Could it be that the same Avraham—who survived Nimrod's fiery furnace and would later be willing to sacrifice his own son—was actually undecided about following God's command? There must be something more to the story.

It is certainly human to consider reasons for turning away from the path that leads us to being Godly. And from that consideration can grow great resolve in our commitment to following the correct path. This interaction, though, is not just about Avraham; the voices of these men are voices in each of us.

Aner is afraid of pain. We know this guy well. He's the part of us that resists any action that involves discomfort, the one who would sooner be alone than put in the effort to build and keep a relationship.

Eshkol doesn't want to be different. He's the part of us that likes to blend in. He's the reason we won't say a blessing out loud in public or dance with abandon on Simchat Torah.

Then there's Mamre. Mamre doesn't deny the existence of pain or the discomfort of being different; he simply focuses on the bigger picture. Mamre doesn't even talk about the meaning of the commandment, the opportunity to elevate even our most physical activities to a spiritual realm. He just reminds Avraham to trust that God knows best. Mamre is the part of us that is unafraid of anything but being far from God. Mamre doesn't discount the arguments against following Hashem's directive; He trumps them.

Avraham leaned toward Mamre's words because they reflected the approach Avraham had spent his life developing. The way we lean will very much depend on which aspect we spend time developing. If I make most of my decisions based on what is less painful or less different, I am allowing the concerns of Aner and Eshkol to keep me from my best self. When I involve myself in strengthening my understanding of Hashem and His faith in me through a valid *mesorah*, I will be able to accept the concerns of Aner and Eshkol while inviting the voice of Mamre to resound through my actions.

And then, wherever I await the next growth opportunity, I will be in the "Plains of Mamre."

Without Further Ado

VAYEIRA

"Vayeira—And God appeared."

Just like that.

We cannot see and hear Hashem in our physically limited state of being in this world, so what does it mean that He "appeared" to someone?

- Is it that God made it clear in the person's mind that He was with him?
- Maybe "appearing" is like God saying, "My presence fills the world, and right now, I am letting you feel what it is like to have My complete, intense focus on you."

Hashem's "appearance" teaches us that another's existence provides an opportunity for us to temporarily suspend all else and completely be with someone else. Being with another is not about me. When my friend is sharing her story, I don't need to bring the conversation back to my experience. I can simply listen to her story and give my attention to its importance. This is love and modesty in action.

To practice this focus on the other, you need to know that you are good without having to prove your worth to another. You also need to know that the other person has worth, and that you have the power to remind them of that worth.

With this knowledge—and the determination to rise above instinct—you can appear.

Godly.

Power of Another Kind

CHAYEI SARAH

One evening, shortly after Hurricane Sandy, my husband and I headed to a wedding in Cedarhurst, New York.

The hurricane had left her mark.

We drove slowly through neighborhoods with no streetlamps, past dark, vacant homes abandoned by residents seeking warmth and power. It was like a ghost town. Shops that promised "Open twenty-four hours" were closed. Lightless traffic lights swayed eerily in intersections, with no indication of who should proceed.

As we turned into the darkened parking lot of the wedding hall, we noticed that further down the street, orange blockades kept vehicles from driving where the road had imploded. We made our way by flashlight to the entrance of the shul…and into a most powerful reality.

Candlelight filled the reception area, where the radiant bride enthusiastically greeted her guests. The groom's *tish* rocked with heartfelt singing and uninhibited dancing, mostly from the top-hatted groom himself.

As is often the case when lights are dim, people felt bound to each other more deeply than when bright lights distract our focus to externals, our own and others'. In the small glowing flames, faces were hard to make out, but hearts were clear as day. Every heart had come to celebrate, and without heat, warmth still pervaded.

When Avraham sends Eliezer to find a wife for Yitzchak, he sends him to Aram Naharayim. This was the place steeped in idol worship that Avraham had left years earlier by Hashem's command! What kind of daughter-in-law was Avraham hoping to find?

There is a most profound lesson here. The ground rules in Aram Naharayim were about basic decency and consideration for others. True, the people were confused about how to serve God and actualize their potentials, but that could be learned later. Yet if a person is brought up in a society that lacks basic decency, it will be incredibly difficult for them to become a kind person. In particular, kindness is necessary for the success of any relationship, and Avraham knew this.

One of the gifts Eliezer presents to Rivkah when he realizes that she will be the one to marry Yitzchak is a nose ring that weighed one *beka*. (Rivkah's name is related to this weight, as it shares two root letters with *beka*.) *Rashi* tells us that a *beka* was worth one half-shekel.

Why do we need this information?

The half-shekel is what each Jew would later contribute yearly to the *Mishkan*. They would give a half in order to know they were not whole without giving to and receiving from others. Eliezer's gift therefore hinted to what he saw in Rivkah—kindness—and how this value would later manifest itself in her descendants.

In the aftermath of destruction, we focus on the basics: While our bodies need food, clothing, and shelter, our relationships need kindness. Avraham knew what he was doing when he sent Eliezer out of Canaan. He was stressing what is most important to look for in a mate.

I pray that our friends who wed that night will consistently value the staple of kindness. Those who value kindness can experience infinite power in their relationships, and those relationships create an energy all their own. An electricity flows from the passionate commitment to that kindness.

And then, plenty of light shines even in the darkest places.

Mazel Tov!

CHAYEI SARAH

According to Torah Law, for a union to be defined as a marriage, there are specific criteria that need to be met:

- The partners must be Jewish human beings.
- One individual must be a man, and one a woman.
- The two must not be siblings, parent/child, or aunt/nephew.
- If the woman was married before, she must have a proper *get* (divorce contract), which was prepared, offered, and accepted according to Jewish law.

There are three necessary parts of a Jewish lawful wedding: *erusin, kiddushin, nesu'in*.

Additionally:

- Two witnesses sign the *ketubah* (halachic marriage contract).
- The man gives the woman an item worth at least a *perutah*, usually a ring.
- The woman accepts the item.
- There are two *shomer Shabbat* witnesses.

- The *ketubah*, which binds the man to marital obligations, is held by the man, who offers it to the woman.
- The woman accepts the *ketubah*.
- The man and woman are alone together in a *yichud* room.
- Following the festivities, the marriage is privately consummated.

Then there are laws of *taharat ha'mishpachah*, which maintain dignity and renewal throughout the marriage. There are so many details to ensure a proper marriage, and yet legal bindings alone do not a lasting marriage create.

In *Parashat Chayei Sarah*, Avraham sends his servant, Eliezer, to find a wife for his son, Yitzchak. There was no Jdate or eHarmony—there were people, camels, and wells. And Eliezer had one very specific criterion: kindness. Avraham wanted his daughter-in-law to possess kindness, the kind of kindness that is a conscious second nature.

It's easy to show kindness when we're feeling rested, fed, pampered, and unhurried. The challenge of being kind arises in the small day-to-day interactions in the midst of our busyness. Like, when we plan to just pop over to the supermarket to pick up a cold drink, and we end up waiting in line behind ten other people. Or we head over to the well just to fetch a pail of water, and a thirsty man with ten camels shows up. Those moments test the strength of our kindness.

The legally bound spouses are living on quicksand if they are living without kindness. Kindness is the foundation of any meaningful, lasting relationship, and long lives deep kindness when it settles in prioritized boundaries. When kindness is harnessed and consciously given in such a way that the most consistent dose is given to my spouse, then to my children, then parents, then family, then friends, then others, the kindness grows as a tended-to garden.

When I care for myself daily in such a way that allows me to maintain a pretty good semblance of these priorities, I am continuously nourishing the roots of that foundation of kindness. If we are kind without prioritizing, in time we will lose ourselves. We will become resentful of those who want our kindness. A kind character is developed over time. It is found superficially in those who display random acts of sensitivity. It is found deeply in those who also tend to their kindness with *gevurah* (discipline).

Avraham knew that his son, Yitzchak, was quite self-disciplined, and Yitzchak needed someone who strongly exemplified *chessed* (kindness). That would be Rivkah. At the same time, Rivkah needed Yitzchak for his ability to maintain boundaries.

This yin-yang idea is not reserved for two separate beings alone. As seemingly opposing forces can complement each other in a marriage, so it is cause for celebration when we accept and cultivate both forces within ourselves.

So mazel tov! To all who work to marry these two character traits within themselves!

Simchahs!

In All Fairness

TOLDOT

"It's not fair!"

How often have I heard this refrain?

From my students, probably most days that I taught in the classroom. From my children, at least once a week for the past two decades, and still going.

A child's definition of "fair":

- When I have the same—or more—good stuff as/than everyone else.

An adult's definition of "fair":

- When everyone has what they've worked for.

God's definition of "fair":

- When each person has the opportunities that he/she needs in order to be his/her best self—which only God knows.

If I think that my mission in parenting is to make everything fair according to my child's definition of fair, I am teaching my child that her definition is correct. In an effort to ease my immediate discomfort of hearing a complaining child, I am cheating my child out of learning the ultimate concept of fairness.

The Torah introduces us to twins, Yaakov and Eisav.

- Yaakov grows up to be Godly.
- Eisav grows to be far from Godly.

In Godly fairness, Eisav must have had the opportunity to overcome his negative leanings. It must be that Hashem endowed Eisav with the character and ability to become his most Godly self. While Hashem, in all "fairness," will provide the seeds needed for one to be his best self, parents can either help or hinder the growth of their children.

According to Rabbi Hirsch, Yitzchak's "fairness" hindered Eisav's growth. The boys were brought up in the same manner, which would seem to be a fair approach.

Yet Rabbi Hirsch shares something profound: Yitzchak treated the boys as if they had the same character. The traditional mode of *chinuch* (education) worked well for Yaakov, but Eisav needed a different track.

Eisav needed an outing, while Yaakov needed a book. Is that fair?

Wouldn't Yaakov complain about that?

Maybe.

But still, complaints do not obligate us to change our minds; only to be empathic, solidify our values, and deliver with stronger love and clarity.

So when a child cries, "It's not fair!" we can respond with a simple, "Yes, according to your calculations, it's not fair." Then we continue to provide for our children according to their needs.

And pray that we serve in Hashem's plan of ultimate fairness.

Broken Crayons

VAYEITZEI

Did you know that broken crayons are better than whole ones?

We don't intentionally purchase broken crayons. Still, I'm telling you... they're better!

In the Torah portion of *Vayeitzei*, our forefather Yaakov encounters endless brokenness:

- The midrash tells us that Yaakov was nearly killed by Eisav's son, Elifaz, who ends up taking all Yaakov's clothing and belongings.
- Lavan's home is far from a healthy working environment. There, payment and marriage do not materialize as promised.
- Lavan's deceit knows no bounds as he continues in his attempts to dupe our forefather throughout his twenty-year stay in Charan.

Would an easier setup have been better?

Perhaps we need to start with a more basic question: What makes one thing better than another? To answer that, we need to know if there is an objective source of "better." And to know that, we need to know if there is an objective source of "good" and "bad."

If good is what feels better or what looks better, then I will concede that anything broken cannot be better. And yet, when I read of a woman who allows her handicapped child to push himself out of his wheelchair in the playground and, without the use of his legs, pull himself up onto a climbing frame and fall and get up over and over again, cut and bleeding and grunting and sweating, much to the discomfort of other park-benched parents, what is that?

How can a loving parent stand by and watch her child struggle in pain and anguish? Isn't it better to keep the child safe and warm?

And when that same child successfully reaches the top, and triumphantly shouts through his tears, "I did it...Mommy...I did it! I love you!" what then?

Do we still think that keeping the child safe and warm is better? It certainly would "look" better. Brokenness does not look good, but fear of it can keep us from our better selves. Even the "whole" child needs to be given space to fall and break a little if he is to grow.

> Even the "whole" child needs to be given space to fall and break a little if he is to grow.

Muscles are built when they are stretched until they tear. Then they repair themselves with stronger fibers. Hashem hands us brokenness, and we can choose to remain undeveloped by not using what is broken toward any purpose. Alternatively, we can be like Yaakov, who pulled himself through brokenness to build himself, his family, and the foundation for the future of our people.

In order to build, we must be willing to pull together lots of brokenness, like our friend from the wheelchair.

When I heard of a friend, a spiritually sensitive Jewish young man, who is engaged to a lovely girl who is not Jewish, I was crestfallen! How does this thinking man find himself on the verge of abandoning a value he previously espoused as crucial to meaningful Jewish continuity? What we claim to value has no worth until our actions speak of that value. And actions necessitate effort, and effort invites breakage.

I picture our friend clinging to what feels easy, as if sitting in a wheelchair. It feels good to sit there right now—no sweat, no tears, and he even has pleasant company. He has decided that committing to the ideal of marrying within the faith is not worth the effort.

Studies of development in preschool-age children show that because small crayon stubs cannot be grasped in a clenched fist, but must be finger-tip held, they are better for building fine motor skills. The drawing made with whole crayons may turn out looking the same as the one created from crayon bits—and the child who moved from his wheelchair may sit on the same rung as his physically fit peer. Yet there is a world of difference in the process of drawing that picture or reaching that rung. The person who breaks away from the circumstances that leave him undeveloped and decides to move into circumstances where growth is more likely may look just like the individual who simply found himself in that place. And yet the inner space of the one who broke himself in the process has expanded beyond measure.

Whole crayons leave little fingers less developed. If we want to grow, we must value and utilize those broken crayons for as long as we can still draw from them.

Absolutely!

VAYEITZEI

She called herself a "relativist." And she wanted my advice. She had a two-year old child and told me that she didn't know how to handle him while maintaining her personal beliefs.

I did not understand.

"For example," she explained, "he wants to stay in the toy store when I'm ready to leave."

I said, "That sounds right."

Then she told me about how that was the whole problem. She couldn't bring herself to make him leave just because she wanted to go. She believed her son was just as right as she was. Apparently, being a relativist means that nobody is more right than anybody else. And if she was going to be true to her beliefs, she could not tell her two-year-old son what to do!

I have no idea how she ever left the store—or did anything, for that matter. (Did she tell the store owner that he had no right closing the store when her child wanted it to remain open?) How unsettling for that child! How confusing! How insensitive will that child be to the needs of others! There was no advice I could give that would have been heard here. If you don't believe that there is a concept of absolute right and wrong, there is nowhere to go. (Except to the toy store, apparently.)

Argue with me about what those absolutes are. Disagree with me. Struggle with restrictions and contradictions. But don't tell me there are no absolute rights and wrongs.

Our forefather Yaakov studied for fourteen years in the school of Shem and Ever to prepare himself for life with Lavan. He had to know with clarity what was right and what was wrong so as not to be influenced by Lavan's worldview:

"There is no right and wrong; only what feels good to me and what doesn't feel good to me. My decisions and manipulations are based on the feel-good outcome."

Kinda like that two-year-old.

Kinda like the two-year-old in all of us.

A child needs firm, clear, loving guidance. A child needs to know there is right and wrong for his safety and character development. And as that child (in each of us) grows into a sensitive, thoughtful, kind human being, he can thank God he's not a relativist!

At a Loss

VAYISHLACH

The Torah is not primarily a history book. It is a guide to life, which usually follows the course of history. The Torah is lessons, morals, and instructions—for all time.

A midrash: Yitzchak leaves his possessions to both sons, Yaakov and Eisav. Eisav makes a logical proposition. "Let's divide all our father's possessions, and since I am the oldest twin, I'll choose what I want. You'll have the other half."

Yaakov proposes a different split. "One of us will take all of Father's fortune (cattle, gold, silver, servants...). The other will have Me'arat Hamachpeilah (the Double Cave, where the Patriarchs and Matriarchs are buried) and Eretz Yisrael."

Yaakov tells Eisav. "Choose which one you want."

The end of the midrash is predictable, right? Obviously, Eisav will choose all the material goods. Yet there's a twist. Before rendering a decision, Eisav goes to ask advice from Yishmael's son, Nevayot.

Nevayot considers the fact that Israel is presently inhabited by Canaanites, and there is no telling when Eisav would actually get to live in the land as his own. The convincing argument is the fact that the material possessions have immediate benefit.

Eisav follows the advice and signs a contract stating that Eretz Canaan (Israel), including the Machpeilah, belongs to Yaakov and his children forever. (Wouldn't it be great to find that contract now?!)

While I am tempted to dwell on the fact that Eisav is all about "now" and "me," I am fascinated by the idea that Eisav sought advice on this one! What drew him to seek counsel? Was he possibly interested in owning Eretz Yisrael, which he may never have settled during his lifetime? Was he actually considering the possibility of letting Yaakov enjoy all the material possessions? What is going on here?

Eisav was clever. I wonder if Eisav's offer was to test Yaakov: "Let's live by logic and 'this world' fairness! Split the goods evenly, and the older chooses. C'mon, Yaakov. I'm offering you to live by 'this world' fairness! Take it!"

And Yaakov responds: "I do not function by 'this world' logic, and you know it, Eisav. A fair split in my eyes is between material and spiritual. Let's do it that way. And you choose: Own what will connect you directly to God. Otherwise, own the rest."

The fact that Eisav doesn't respond immediately tells us Eisav was torn. Perhaps he actually wanted the connection to God? If this was the case, though, why seek counsel from Yishmael's family? If you seek spirituality, you find a source of spiritual living. But it doesn't seem plausible that Eisav was leaning in that direction. We do not see any indication of Eisav being interested in representing God. So why might he have been torn? Why did he seek advice?

We know Eisav desired the material world—all of it. But he was willing to part from some of it—if he could get Yaakov to lower his standards. Evil not only wants it all; it wants nobody else to get their way. Perhaps Eisav sought advice to resolve this dilemma:

- Do I take the fortune and let Yaakov get what he wants?
- Or do I take what Yaakov wants, even though I have no use for it, simply to ensure that my brother will not get what he wants?

Eisav can't figure out how to win this one. He desperately wants to get what he wants *and* prevent Yaakov from getting his way! He seeks out cousin Nevayot who might have said something like this: "Eisav, you function in the here and now. Yaakov's offer is not logical. It's about God and the future. There's no practical way to prevent him from getting what he wants because really, he doesn't want anything tangible. The land is just a representation of his true desire—to pass down a connection to God for his descendants to inherit. No choice you make will take that away from him. Even if you choose the land, your children will not want it. Yaakov's children will figure out a way to get it because they want it. You can't make Yaakov lose, but at least if you choose the "stuff," you'll get something now! It's not everything you want; it's a consolation prize, but it's the bed you've made. You can't win."

Interestingly, traditional sources tell us that Yishmael did *teshuvah* (repentance) in his old age. He personally came close to God. Still, Yishmael's *teshuvah* did not influence the trajectory of his descendants. While it can be too late to change the effects of our past behavior on those around us, it's never too late to change ourselves. And maybe Yaakov's offer to Eisav was a last-ditch effort to remind Eisav that the power to choose was still in his hands.

Otherwise Yaakov could have just said, "Cut the garbage, Eisav! I know you want all the material goods. You know I want the land. Let's just split it, and I'll be on my way."

But no, Yaakov presents the option as Eisav's choice. The Gemara relates that, years later, when Yaakov's body is about to be buried in Me'arat Hamachpeilah, Eisav stops the procession claiming that the last space in the cave is reserved for him.

One of Yaakov's twelve sons, Naftali, runs back to Egypt to procure the original contract. In the meantime, Chushim, Dan's son, who's deaf, is upset that Eisav seems to be holding up Zeidy's burial. With swift force, Chushim bashes Eisav's head, and Eisav dies there, on his brother's coffin. *Pirkei D'Rabi Eliezer* adds that Eisav's head rolled into Me'arat Hamachpeilah, and his body was buried in Har Se'ir. Perhaps Eisav had thoughts of connecting to God, yet he never lived them.

We are Yaakov's descendants. While we live with materialism, we can know what is eternal. We can act on that knowledge and seek counsel from the upright. Those who are energized by eternity are the winners. In every generation.

After the Mourning

VAYEISHEV

Ten brothers walked together. They carried the cloak of their father's favorite son, which was covered in blood. They showed it to their father and asked if he recognized the garment.

He did. And he mourned.

The word for mourning in Hebrew is *aveilut*. The root is *aval*, which connotes "exception," as in, "I feel good, but (*aval*) I could be better." Rabbi Hirsch notes a connection between mourning and the word *aval*. When a loved one dies, it is proper to mourn. It is proper to feel, "I am living, but (*aval*) my loved one is gone." When the fact that my loved one is gone looms larger than the fact that I am alive, that is *aveilut*, mourning. When *aveilut* is over, it is time to focus on the first fact—the fact that I am alive. It's time to minimize the "*aval*."

Each of us, in every moment, can mourn. I can feel a lacking and decide that because

> Each of us, in every moment, can mourn. I can feel a lacking and decide that because of what I lack, I cannot be happy.

of what I lack, I cannot be happy. *Aval* can undermine that which precedes it. As long as there is *aval*, there is sadness. You may say there is always *aval*, and indeed there is: I have accomplished much, *but* there is still so much to do!

We live in *galut* (exile), and the ultimate redemption will usher in a whole new reality. All mourning will cease. I will say, "I am alive," without an *aval*. That will be then.

So what to do today? The excuses for me to be continuously in mourning exist, and many are valid. Is there a way to live with peace of mind in *galut*?

Rabbi Avigdor Miller lists ten steps to greatness. One of the steps is to take a minute each day, in private, to sit and mourn the loss of Yerushalayim.

One minute.

In the other moments, in the other days, we need to replace the *aval*. Instead of *but* we can say *and*.

- "I am alive, *and* my loved one is gone."
- "I feel good, *and* I could be better."

By replacing the *aval*, I create a space for acceptance of circumstance. I accept that there will always be a reason not to reach for joy. *And* I can still reach for joy. I can choose to move beyond a constant state of mourning, even as the reasons to remain there hang over me and threaten to drown me.

Let them threaten. Let them hang. *And* I will live. Without *aval*.

Owning
My Conscience

MIKETZ

When I was ten, I called a rabbi "stupid." I didn't mean to. It just slipped out. He was giving me and my older brother a ride home after Shabbat. He was acting silly, pretending he didn't know which house was ours, and I blurted out, "You just passed our house, stupid!"

I knew the second that word fell out of my mouth that I had done something horrible. I was mortified. As soon as the car stopped, I bolted into the house, straight to my bedroom, to feel awful by myself. Then I heard my twelve-year-old brother announce, "D'vorah called Rabbi Rodman stupid!" He was clearly reveling in the possibility of my punishment, as he was usually the one in trouble.

My mother came into my room. I couldn't look at her. She sat on my bed. "You need to call and apologize," she stated as a matter of fact.

All I could think was, *I can't.* I just wanted to disappear. The thought of making that phone call seemed impossible to me. Impossible.

My mother sat for a couple more minutes while I repeated my mantra: *I can't, I can't, I can't...*

I don't recall any conversation on the matter.

Just my feeling of dread, my mantra, and the knowledge that I *was* going to make that call. The next scene in my mind: I'm holding the phone in my parents' bedroom.

I dial.

The rabbi answers. I say, "This is D'vorah Lerner. I'm sorry for what I said in the car."

Silence. And then...

I hear a smile on the other end, perhaps a chuckle, and, "I forgive you."

I say, "Thank you," and I hang up.

At first, I feel a little more awful. I cry a little and do a shaky jig around the room in an effort to move past the lingering discomfort. End of memory.

In *Parashat Miketz*, Yosef faces his brothers. As events unfold, Yosef does not save his brothers from the discomfort that follows the realization of their wrongdoing in the sale of Yosef years earlier. He wants his brothers' *teshuvah* to be complete.

Then began the dawning of hearing their own consciences. The distress of leaving Shimon imprisoned, finding the money in Levi's sack, having to bring Binyamin to Egypt, and then finding the goblet in his sack. Each of these harrowing experiences was an opportunity to raise the brothers' consciousness. The discomfort of dining with Yosef was to remind them of how comfortable they had been to feast after the sale of Yosef. They needed to feel their own discomfort for their *teshuvah* to be proper. Being with our own discomfort is an opportunity.

On that Saturday night, my mother gave me a great allowance. She allowed me to feel my own discomfort in recognizing my wrong. I carried my own embarrassment and fear, and then I could do what was right. Not because my mother might be embarrassed, but just because I needed to do the right thing. My mother did not attempt to demean me; she only provided the space for me to feel bad within the understanding that I would do *teshuvah*. Not because I was bad, rather simply because I had done wrong. There is a right response to wrongdoing, and the right response doesn't always feel good right away.

In fact, it usually feels worse before it feels better, which is sometimes on the other side of a shaky jig.

Who Cares

VAYIGASH

Society has created a monster called tolerance.

What may have been born as acceptance of differences within the realm of an absolute moral standard has become acceptance of and excuses for almost all behavior. Gone are days of teaching absolutes in terms of acceptable behavior. The Western world has become obsessed with the idea of tolerance above all.

Efraim and Menasheh were Yosef's sons, and they were born and bred in Egypt. Jewish boys are blessed every Friday night to be like Efraim and Menasheh. Hold that thought.

A group of university students was asked: If you were on an island where human sacrifice was about to take place, would you attempt to stop it? Unbelievably, most students said no. They said that they would not interfere with that tribal custom!

There is a murder about to take place, and tolerance compels you to not only allow it but to see it as a valid practice?! This is sick! This is what comes of a society raised and educated on the false premise that there is no evil.

Live and let die. As the tolerance monster grows, so grows passivity and indifference.

"You can you do whatever you want," basically means, "I don't care." As opposed to:

- "I care about you because you were created in God's image."
- "I want you to live life to the fullest."
- "While I know that ultimately I can only control my own thoughts and behavior, I can still be a light to you, a source of motivation and guidance should you choose to move in the right direction."

And yes, there is a right direction. And no, I will not say, "Do whatever you want; it's your life." Do you know why? Because I don't want to tolerate you! I tolerate pain, and I don't want to see you as a pain. I want to care about you! I want to care in a way that the all-tolerant never can.

> I don't want to tolerate you! I tolerate pain, and I don't want to see you as a pain. I want to care about you!

We bless our boys to be like Yosef's sons, who were raised in a society with alternative lifestyles and beliefs. Sound familiar? Efraim and Menasheh were surrounded by the concept of broken boundaries, yet they retained their father's sense of right and wrong. That is why we bless our sons to be like them.

Yosef cared for others. He contemplated and implemented a plan to save Egypt from starvation. His life was not about tolerance; it was about caring enough to take action. When we state unapologetically that there are absolute lines between right and wrong, we can state emphatically that each human life is sacred.

And we can care enough to actively make a difference in the lives of others.

Get Together!

VAYECHI

We ran a couples workshop, my husband and I. Twenty married people (plus cookies).

Each couple was different. Each marriage was different. Yet we all agreed on the same fundamental principles of a lasting relationship. And we all agreed that a marriage will not last without effort. What is the motivation to make the effort? Valuing connection over comfort.

We admire people who overcome great obstacles with great effort. We can admire ourselves for doing the same.

In *Parashat Vayechi*, we read that our forefather Yaakov is about to pass away. He calls for his sons, the twelve tribes. "Assemble yourselves," he says. "Gather yourselves and listen," he says. Before he begins to tell them about the future and bless them, he is saying, "Get together!"

Why did God make twelve distinct tribes? Why not just one big homogeneous family? The same reason He made people different: We have to work to get along. We have to put in effort to find ways to connect, and through our efforts, we become stronger, better people.

I can take this from Yaakov's message to his children: The strength that grows from putting in the effort to connect is, in itself, our future and our blessing.

Of Strength and a Reverend

VAYECHI

"If I find something to be in error after careful study and research, I will change, regardless of the cost."

Baptist Minister J. David Davis, Tennessee, 1981

At the conclusion of the communal reading of the book of *Bereishit*:

- Ashkenazim in shul proclaim: *"Chazak, chazak v'nitchazek*—Be strong, be strong, and we'll be strengthened!"
- Sephardim congratulate each other with the words *"Chazak u'baruch*—Be strong and blessed," following each *aliyah* to the Torah. Then the *oleh*, the one who got the *aliyah*, replies, *"Chazak v'amatz*—Be strong and brave."

We are continuously reminded that we need strength when it comes to Torah.

J. David Davis was a Baptist minister who ventured into taboo territory by questioning the validity of specific Christian teachings. His unanswered questions led him and his congregation out of mainstream Christianity and into Torah living as Noachides. He chronicles his journey in the book *Finding the God of Noah*. Through Torah study, Written and Oral, Davis discovered what God really wants from mankind.

"*Etz chayim hi*"—the Torah is our life, "*lamachazikim bah*—to those who grasp it." However, for those who merely read it without holding onto it, Torah is a burden.

A parable: A community of people live just beyond a vast desert. The only way to cross the desert is on foot. Whenever visitors arrive, they are carrying the barest minimum of provisions, and they are exhausted. One day an energetic man arrives, carrying a heavy case. The townspeople are dumbfounded!

"How is it that you are so full of life despite schlepping that luggage? Why did you not discard it along the way?"

The man answers, "I am so full of life because of what I carry!" He pulls out a violin from his bag and begins playing beautiful music. "This is what keeps me going! If I were to discard it, I would surely be finished."

The violin is the Torah. It is something to carry, and at the same time, it carries us. "*Chazak*" encourages us to focus on the ultimate benefits of grasping and utilizing the instrument of Torah.

We are human. We are tempted to follow the path of least resistance—to drop the luggage. Reverend Davis came to the truth of Torah. This gave him a new burden to carry, but he carried it, as he promised he would.

When the individuals are strong, so will be the community. Since Hashem's world is raised through interdependence, our commitment and that of others matters to us. Reverend Davis's quest to live within truth brings the world closer to the ultimate revelation.

After *Bereishit*, we begin the book of *Shemot*, a new chapter in the history of the Jewish People. A chapter of unbearable pain, loss, and struggle, but a necessary process in our becoming the "light unto the nations," and a template of all struggles to come.

We need the message of "*Chazak*" to resound as we venture into this reading. Without resolve to learn and take to heart, mind, and action the teachings of the Torah, we are doomed to live without conviction. Without change.

When a Jew would ask Reverend J. David Davis, leader of the Emmanuel Noachide congregation in Athens, Tennessee, "Why don't you convert? Why don't you live as a Jew?" he would answer, "As a gentile following God's expectations of me, I am fulfilling my place in God's scheme of the world." Then, he would often challenge the questioner, "Why don't *you* live as a Jew?"

Indeed.

Chazak, chazak, v'nitchazek!

SHEMOT

Enjoy the View!

SHEMOT

When you are in a good place, the view is clear. When you have an unobstructed vantage point, the scene can be breathtaking.

Miriam crouched in the reeds along the Nile river. She kept her eyes on that wicker basket, on the child in that basket, her brother. She knew with certainty that this brother would be the savior of the Jewish People, yet she did not know how that would play out.

Curious as to the workings of God in this world, Miriam found a good place to watch the events unfold. Would she have ever guessed that Pharaoh's daughter would be the one to find the basket? How many questions must have arisen in her mind as to what would happen next. Would the baby be taken to the palace? How would he grow to be the Jewish leader from there?

Miriam was a prophetess. She already knew this child's fate, but she did not know the details of the plot. How exactly would his fate play out? What road would be laid before him? She also did not know what role she would have in the story. While she waited in wonderment, she also kept a lookout for her next opportunity to be an active player in the story. As soon as Miriam noticed the baby crying and the princess's inability to soothe him, Miriam was on the move. Opportunity arose, and she sprang into action.

We are not prophets. We do not know the ending of any individual story in this world. Still, we do know that the ultimate end of everything is good. When we remember that, we have a good vantage point. And as we go about our days, we can watch with simple curiosity, marvel at events as they unfold, and wait to spring at each opportunity as it arises. Then, we'll be utilizing our faith to play a starring role in God's plan.

Be Long in Spirit

SHEMOT

You've had a long, hard day. At the moment, all you want is a hot shower and some good food. You feel this way pretty often nowadays. There was a time when you had dreams and aspirations and hopes for a bigger life. You used to feel happier to be alive. Recently, though, life has been so hectic, and you've been so overwhelmed. Your positive attitude has been replaced with thoughts of simply surviving each day.

Today, something happens. You get a call from the CEO of that company you once dreamed of working for. He says he's heard great things about you, and he wants to hire you. He just wants you to listen to what it means to work for his company.

Are you still exhausted? Do you still only want to get through the day? Are you unwilling to listen to his words? Or do you find yourself suddenly energized with a new spirit, a new hope and excitement, an eagerness to know more? As long as you have continuously chosen to leave space in your life for a spirit of hope to reside, you will notice and respond with optimism when growth opportunities arise. On the contrary, if you are completely enslaved to the demands of your daily life, stuck in the daily grind, you may be too tired to listen when a calling presents itself.

The Jewish People were stuck in a rut. They were in Mitzrayim, literally translated as "straits." They were not just exhausted in body; they were exhausted in spirit. The physical labor was so constant that there was no time to think, to dream, or to hope. When Moshe came to tell the Jews that he had been sent by Hashem Himself to lead them out of Egypt, the *pasuk* says, "They did not listen to Moshe from shortness of spirit and hard work."[1]

> As long as you have continuously chosen to leave space in your life for a spirit of hope to reside, you will notice and respond with optimism when growth opportunities arise.

"*Kotzer ruach*—Shortness of spirit," is written first. Had they simply been physically worn out, they might have found the energy to hear the opportunity they had once dreamed about, longed for, and hoped to experience. However, their spirit was "short." It had not been given space to grow, so they could not feel the thrill of the opportunity at hand.

To avoid being *kotzer ruach*, we need to prioritize our time and feed our minds positive thoughts. Yes, we have a myriad of obligations in a day, but we also have the freedom to make time for what is important, and we have brain space enough to keep our spirits alive. We can decide to spend the drive to work or school focused on all the annoyances and drudgery of the tasks that lie ahead. Or we can find ways to open our minds and hearts to the joy of living and the possibilities for goodness that lie ahead.

Will we let Pharaoh dictate our headspace? Or will we let the opportunities that Moshe represents play out in our minds? Today, will I be enslaved to negative thoughts and exhausting worries? Or will I work to free my mind from that bondage and focus on spirit-strengthening ideas so that I will recognize and reach for invitations of growth opportunities?

---

1   *Shemot* 6:9.

If I am tired just thinking about choosing the latter, I've got to figure out how to redesign my day so I can embrace the choice that positively redefines my existence.

Today.

All's Fair in God's Mercy

VA'EIRA

Pharaoh is an interesting character. Right at the beginning of the *parashah*, he "doesn't know" Yosef.

Seriously? Even if he wasn't the same Pharaoh who appointed Yosef to save Egypt from famine, not remembering doesn't fly. That's like the president of South Africa in seventeen years not remembering Nelson Mandela!

The Pharaoh in this story is resisting goodness, and as we get to know him, he's resisting *teshuvah*. The opportunity to do *teshuvah* is a gift. To reflect on our actions, to regret wrongdoings, to make amends, to change. It's a chance to move closer to goodness.

Teshuvah entered the world with the first sin. We needed it because Man could not live on justice alone. *Teshuvah* is born out of God's mercy, and because of our limitations, *teshuvah* is a process in which we are to be involved constantly. It's about our relationship with Hashem, and our desire, struggle, and commitment to be in that intimate relationship. And, like marriage, *teshuvah* can be encouraged but not coerced. Let's look at what happened with Pharaoh's heart to better understand the concept of *teshuvah* opportunities. Pharaoh hardened his own heart, then God hardened Pharaoh's heart. There are two ways to acquire a hardened heart: passively and actively.

- A person can passively allow his heart to harden into a depressing, cynical mass of negativity. This can happen easily to one who avoids taking responsibility for his or her own growth.
- One can actively harden his heart by deciding to represent the antithesis of Godliness.

With Pharaoh, it was not just that he was uninspired; he was hellbent on being uninspired! His hardened heart did not grow from laziness—he was active in his desire to be evil. This may have been enough to earn the "punishment" of God hardening Pharaoh's heart because, after all, *"B'derech she'adam rotzeh leileich*—[God helps] a man in the way he wants to go."

- Okay, you dug in your heels here? God will pour the cement over them now.
- You've closed the door to your made-up mind? God will lock it.

But what about *teshuvah*? Where is the opportunity for repentance here? Is there really a point of no return?

I once heard an explanation on this idea from Rabbi Yaakov Ciment. God is fair, he explained. When God hardened Pharaoh's heart, he was leveling the playing field. Pharaoh was human, and he could only harden his own heart so much. His own hardening of his heart was no match for the revelation of God's omnipotence through the plagues. Witnessing the plagues would have been too powerful an experience for Pharaoh to ignore with his own hardened heart. Pharaoh would have involuntarily recognized the Creator and done His Will. But he would have been doing coerced *teshuvah*—not true *teshuvah*.

Hashem balanced the scales of choice for Pharaoh to enable him to do absolute *teshuvah*, which the midrash says he ultimately did and more. Pharaoh eventually saw his entire kingdom destroyed, and at the Yam

Suf, he watched his army drown. Like an addict in denial, he had to hit rock bottom before he finally turned around. Still, this was the active Pharaoh! The midrash reveals that he traveled to Nineveh, where he eventually became the king who, after hearing dire predictions from the prophet Yonah, directed that city through the *teshuvah* process.

Our playing fields are level, and there is balance in the forces of our personal world. Faith in God's fairness, and an appreciation for the gift of *teshuvah*, can keep us on track.

Signs of Life

BO

"A Jew who does not believe in miracles is not a realist."

I have read that this was said by David Ben Gurion. I have also read variations of the quote. No matter; this idea works for the message today. Miracles abound at the time of the Exodus. In Hebrew, *nes* is a "miracle," and it also means a "sign" or a "banner."

If you cross the Hudson River over the Tappan Zee bridge, you'll see a sign: "Life is worth living."

Then, another sign: "When it seems there's no hope, there is help."

At first, I think the State of New York is encouraging positive thinking and unity. Sweet. Then, I think again. These signs are on a bridge— a high bridge.

People jump from high bridges. My thinking slowly turns to sadness. I wonder how many people took their lives here before the city decided to post encouraging words in the hopes of preventing the next deadly jump. Then I wonder how many lives, if any, are saved by those signs. At the moment a man stands on the ledge, he is trapped in his overwhelming desperation. He is enslaved to his sense of wanting to end it all.

"And surely your blood of your lives will I require."[1] The understanding of this verse is the injunction against suicide, and the law prohibiting suicide must be learned by those on firm ground, far from bridge ledges. There, "Do not take your own life" is as bottom line as "Do not steal" and "Do not murder."

"And you will guard very much, for your lives"[2] is a positive commandment to care for ourselves. This, too, is for acceptance on firm ground, so that we, who are on the ground, may learn these rules. Do not take your life—guard your life.

If we are to distance ourselves far from the desperation that leads a man to end his own life, it is good to know what constitutes firm ground. In *Parashat Bo*, two positive mitzvot were fulfilled before the redemption:

- *brit milah* (circumcision)
- *korban Pesach* (Passover offering)

Milah is a sign on the body. It is about the individual being bound to God, Who is Infinite. One's personal worldly pursuits are elevated when that individual knows that those pursuits are bound to the Infinite. The blood of the *korban Pesach*—like today's mezuzah—is a sign on the home. It is about binding the family and the community to God. Our homes are elevated when we care enough to bring God into them.

Brit milah is personal, while *korban Pesach* (mezuzah) is familial. Both remind us of our intrinsic value, and both stimulate the growth of firm ground on which we accept God's law. To be redeemed from the bondage of Mitzrayim—from whatever holds us back from living as our best selves—we need to display personal responsibility for our connection to God.

And we need to show familial responsibility. Both. Consistently. Not perfectly, but consistently.

In *Pirkei Avot*, we learn, "If I am not for myself, who am I? And when I am only for myself, what am I?" Who am I? What am I? These can

---

1   *Bereishit* 9:5.
2   *Devarim* 4:15.

be introspective inquiries of someone looking to grow, or foreboding thoughts of someone ready to end all possibility for growth. The category we find ourselves in is determined by the distance between our stance and the ledge, and that distance will be massive when we live responsibly as servants of God only. Then there will be no place for enslavement to anything else.

The Jewish People are miraculous. Our existence alone has earned the awe of great minds throughout centuries. And we don't just survive; we survive vigorously, as a family and as individuals. Each of us is a miracle, a banner for the greatness of God.

When we take responsibility to bind ourselves and our families to God, then no matter where we reside, we live on solid ground. And we become the embodiment of vital signs of life.

Blame It on the Parashah

BO

One evening, one of our teenage daughters makes an announcement about her friend's grandmother. "Mrs. Katz freezes Pesach food from one year to the next. As soon as one Pesach is over, she cooks and bakes for the next one, while her kitchen is still kosher for Pesach."

My kids' out-loud response: "That's sooo gross…year-old food! Yuck!"

My silent thought: *That's crazy!*

Then I tell the kids that the food may possibly be delicious, and not to speak so quickly. And I remind them of one of our house rules regarding food: "Make fun of it? You don't get to eat it!" In my house, I passed this bill into law years ago because I was annoyed by the eye rolling or nose holding that would follow my declaration of what was for supper.

Then I hold back from voicing my mother's mantra: "You mock the thing you are to be." This is a version of "You'll probably end up doing whatever you say you'll never do."

Well, lately, not only am I not mocking, I am actually considering the idea that Pesach prep way in advance is not as crazy as I had previously thought. This week, I bought some things for Pesach. Yes, I know it's still January, and Pesach is in April. It is not something logical, although when my husband asks what the canned goods in the basement cabinet are for, I will state simply, without flinching, "Pesach," as if that is clearly reasonable and obvious. I have practiced this reply to the point that I can make the word "Pesach" sound like "Duh!"

I didn't know why I was feeling such a strong desire to be prepared for Pesach until I began to review the *parashah*. These weeks have been leading us up to *yetziat Mitzrayim* (the Exodus). The weekly Torah portion is teasing me! Of course, now it makes sense: I am yearning for freedom, because I am learning of freedom.

I blame it on the *parashah*!

As the snow continues to drift through New England, we are far from out of the woods of winter. We have just arrived at the Hebrew month of Shevat. On the fifteenth, Rosh Hashanah for the trees, we will celebrate the idea of hope.

In Adar, we will increase our level of happiness by consciously recognizing Hashem's hand in our daily lives, and we'll celebrate Purim. After that, we'll head into the month of Nissan, by which time we'll be fully prepared to tap into our capacity to be free from that which holds us back from being our best selves.

Then we'll arrive at Pesach!

So if I'm doing this in the proper order, it's:

- Shevat—hope
- Adar—happiness
- Nissan—freedom

It's still early. There's still plenty of time to party with the leaven family. I will endeavor to keep that in mind as my mind simultaneously wanders to the basement, where the clandestine canned goods with Kosher for Passover labels lay dormant, awaiting a charge—a purpose.

When can I start cooking and freezing? How soon won't put me in the category of becoming what I labeled "crazy"? How soon won't bring the

children to comment in a way that would disqualify them from partak
ing of the Pesach fare? Clearly, I am obsessing.

Soon we will encounter the time of the actual Exodus and splitting
of the sea. That reminds me of springtime and warm weather. Hmm,
maybe I can convince my husband to take the kids to the beach.

Husband: "Honey, why are these flip-flops piled up at the door?"

Me: "Oh, the ones next to the snow boots? Yeah, those are for the kids
to wear to the beach."

(Duh!)

Freedom from Independence

BESHALACH

Lance Brown was an ex-convict. Soon after being released from prison for bank robbery, he got himself arrested by throwing bricks through windows of federal buildings. Brown said he was homeless and hungry, so he would rather spend time in prison than on the streets.

The Exodus from Egypt is complete! The Jewish People are free! No longer are they enslaved to Pharaoh. And upon this redemption, and on the heels of experiencing the splitting of the sea and having just sung the greatest song of praise to the Almighty, the Jewish People do what? They complain.

They were hungry, so they decided to remember that in Egypt they'd had food. "When we sat by the flesh pots [i.e., BBQs] when we ate bread to satisfaction."[1] This seems a strange memory for the people to have,

---

1   *Shemot* 16:3.

considering the reality of the depth of the oppression from which they had cried out to be released.

One Torah commentator, *Chemdat Hayamim*, goes as far as saying that the people were simply lying, just like a poor man would lie about what he used to enjoy to get others to provide him with that standard. Nechama Leibowitz asks what would prompt the people to lie as such? In Egypt, they had suffered intolerably; how could they possibly even conjure up this blatantly false picture of plenty? She says something that hits like a gut-punch. True, in Egypt the people were worn by suffering and misfortune, but like all slaves, they were free in a certain sense—they were free from taking responsibility for their own destiny—for their own economic and social ordering. The motive of the people's discontent and conjuring up of false memories was to avoid being responsible for their independent lives.

In other words, the people who had just been redeemed by God from physical slavery were afraid to redeem themselves into a world of responsibility. Objectively, this is madness, but subjectively, it makes perfect sense. There is something comfortable about being given orders and being given sustenance and being too restricted to be creative, which could lead to failure.

Taking responsibility for my own life means grappling with limitless options, making decisions, and building relationships that can get messy. It means I stop blaming people and circumstances for my lack of achievement. At the same time, in order to be able to carry the burden of that responsibility, I need to have faith that I can do it, and I need to have friends who remind me of that faith. The newly released Jewish People would take time to grow faith in themselves and each other, and they would take time to grow faith in God.

> Taking responsibility for my own life means grappling with limitless options, making decisions, and building relationships that can get messy. It means I stop blaming people and circumstances for my lack of achievement.

I venture to say that had Lance Brown had faith and friends, he may have made a different choice. We don't need to do a "Lance Brown" to hold ourselves back from being captains of our destinies. We can simply blame and complain. Even in the land of the free and the home of the brave, some choose to shackle themselves to complaining and to cowardly blaming.

I'd rather fly free on the wings of expressed appreciation and courageous responsibility.

With faith and friends, of course.

You're Welcome

YITRO

Soon after we arrived on South African shores and were settling into our new home, twelve-year-old Aaron Altman brought us a very thoughtful gift. It was a "welcome" banner that he had crafted for the school Market Day. I hung it proudly outside our front door and immediately realized its magnificent irony. We were being welcomed with an invitation to welcome others.

In *Parashat Yitro*, Moshe welcomes Yitro to Am Yisrael. The midrash tells us that at the celebratory meal, Moshe would not sit with the guests; he stood and served them. Surely, someone else could have served! Yet Moshe was extending a personal welcome—an extension, a "pay forward" of what had once been done for him.

Flashback: When Moshe had arrived back in Egypt on a mission from God, there was no celebratory meal. There was Aharon, Moshe's brother, welcoming Moshe as a reassurance that he as the older brother harbored no jealousy about the fact that his younger brother would be the leader of the Jewish People. While Aharon certainly could have sent a delegation in his stead, there was something Aharon's live presence

86

could give his brother: a reassurance of his absolute trust that Moshe was the perfect candidate for the position. The effort involved in being the personal welcomer was the clincher. Personal presence creates an energy that reinforces whatever message one is sending to another.

Yitro (Moshe's father-in-law) is praised for not just "hearing" about the miraculous Exodus from Egypt and the splitting of the sea, but for "listening" to the message in what he heard—for paying attention and taking it to heart, mind, and action by leaving his post as priest of Midyan and joining the Jewish nation.

A man may be an excellent troubleshooter. He may notice that nobody is greeting newcomers or that people are hungry. If he simply identifies that people are not being cared for without moving that identification to his heart and action, he is missing out. And so are those who could be benefiting from his actions. That man is not "hearing" the "welcome" in each notice. He is not appreciating that he has been handed a banner.

Yitro heard the welcome. He received the banner. He used it to make himself at home with the chosen nation, where he was personally welcomed by Moshe, who had been personally welcomed by Aharon. Each of us can extend a personal welcome in a way that genuinely invites others into our lives and inspires them to do the same for others.

On Messes and Leaving Home

MISHPATIM

Five-year-olds in cars ask excellent questions.

In his book *Grow the Tree You Got*, Tom Sturges defines an "excellent question" as one to which the questioner does not know the answer. The question from the child in the back seat of the car is, "When Hillel is living away from home, what does he do if he throws up?"

Excellent question. Hillel is our third son, who was, at the time, nineteen years old.

"What, sweetie?" I ask. Not an excellent question. I am just buying processing time.

The child repeats herself.

I answer, "He has to clean it up himself, sweetie girl."

I observe her expression through the rearview mirror. I know what she's thinking: *Wow...That's rough...Another good reason to stay close to home.*

The *parashah* of *Mishpatim* includes laws regarding social interactions—how to live as a responsible member of society, how to treat employees, what to do about damages to property, laws of borrowing and lending, expectations from judges and courts, and settling disputes.

To me, these are ideas about messes and leaving our childhood homes:

- We are ready to leave home when we can clean up our own messes and express appreciation to those who offer assistance. We also need to have shown evidence of the desire and ability to avoid massive messes.
- We are ready to marry when we can help others clean up, people who don't necessarily need our help, but welcome and appreciate it.
- We are ready to have a child when we can clean up after others who absolutely need our help, but do not welcome nor appreciate it.
- We are ready to parent growing children when we can patiently show people how to clean up after themselves, and we can praise them for their efforts.
- We are ready to parent teenagers when we can let them clean up in their own way without undermining their efforts.
- We are ready to let them go when we are confident that they will clean up their own messes, express appreciation to others, and make efforts to avoid massive messes.

It's easy to blame our messes on circumstance and then wait for the cleaning crew to arrive. If we expect to live in a well-functioning society, however, then most of us need to be willing and able to clean up messes, especially ones that we clearly made.

Is that too much to expect from adult members of society?

Un-excellent question.

Uncovering Happiness

MISHPATIM

"When Adar enters we increase simchah."

To increase *simchah*, we need to know what *simchah* is, and we need to possess the tools for acquiring and maintaining it. *Simchah* is usually translated as happiness. The pursuit of happiness can be increasingly fruitless. The pursuit of *simchah*, on the other hand, is increasingly fruitful.

Simchah is a state in which an individual knows that God is involved in his/her life.

It is a place from which I embrace God's will. At the same time that I am disappointed, frustrated, or sad, I can also be *b'simchah*, as long as I hold an awareness of Hashem's involvement in my life. The more open my mind and heart are to this idea, the deeper my level of *simchah* will be.

Parents have tremendous power to influence children in the area of *simchah*. The way in which a parent responds to everyday challenges sets a template for his children to follow. Children can be given the tools to cultivate *simchah*. But what if neither parent offered you the tools? Does that excuse you from being *b'simchah*?

In *Parashat Mishpatim*, we find basic laws for functioning in a social society. As we move from the awesome revelation at Sinai, we go straight into everyday life, where we find a Torah application for every circumstance. *Mishpatim* are rules concerning moral behavior. Nowhere does it say, "If your parents never taught you not to steal, you're off the hook."

Here's the thing. You can be your own parent. In fact, if you hope to become anything you did not become in your parents' home, you *must* be your own parent.

A parent who hopes to instill anything of value in his child needs three objectives:

1. To develop and maintain a loving relationship with the child. Be interested.
2. To be a living example of what he expects from his child. Hold it together when life doesn't turn out as humanly planned.
3. To set clear ground rules and follow through with praise and consequences. Show that actions matter.

We can develop these themes in ourselves and apply as needed when we are parenting our inner child. Each of these three themes can lead us to open ourselves to God in our everyday lives:

1. The first reminds us that Hashem knows and cares about us as individuals.
2. From the second grows understanding that God runs the world.
3. The third can bring us to appreciate why the loving God wants us to follow His law.

Being *b'simchah* as we go about our daily lives may seem an impossible ideal, but idealism is a very real aspect of Torah living. God's expectations of us are ideal. While we often fall short of meeting those expectations, we can grasp the concept that striving for ideal is not useless; every effort in the direction of the ideal is worthy.

Hashem knows our situation. He's completely aware of our struggle to live with a sense of *simchah*. *Pirkei Avot* reminds us: "It is not incumbent on you to finish the work, and you are not free to be excused from it."[1]

---

1   *Pirkei Avot* 2:16.

While on our own we cannot solve every problem, we can figure out how to be part of the solution. A life devoid of *simchah* is a problem. We deserve the chance to live beyond cynicism, and to know *simchat ha'chayim*—the *simchah* of life.

The same God who tells us to believe in Him also commands us to pay for damages, to lend and borrow with consideration, to enjoy physical pleasure in its place, to respect the judicial system, and to return lost property to its owner. This is the same God who tells us to guard Shabbat and keep the festivals. And this same God is involved in our every moment and rooting for our success.

When we decide to know this, we sometimes get to feel the comfort, bliss, and thrill that accompanies that knowledge. Then, all of us, children and adults, get a glimpse of our happiest, Godly selves.

Of Privacy, Slaves, and Selves

MISHPATIM

If a man snuck into someone's property and helped himself to some valuables when nobody was looking, he is called a *ganav*. To pay for his crime, a *ganav* must return the stolen objects or pay their worth. If he is caught with the loot, he must pay double its worth. Alternatively, if he no longer has the objects and has no money to pay, he is sold as a slave so that he can earn money to pay the victim. He then becomes an *eved Ivri*, a "Jewish slave."

Another type of thief is called a *gazlan*. He is a man who stole openly, by force. To pay for his crime, a *gazlan* must return what was stolen or its worth. He does not pay double, and he is not sold as a slave. A *gazlan* cannot become an *eved Ivri*.

The *Shem MiShmuel* explains a significant idea here. Being the Children of Israel means possessing a broad potential for spiritual development. It means knowing that our speech and behavior in private is to be as finely tuned as our public persona because of our awareness of Hashem's constant presence.

The *Shem MiShmuel* brings an example of Moshe Rabbeinu to drive this point home. When Moshe was still living in Pharaoh's palace, he witnessed an argument between two Jews, and he intervened in an attempt to make peace. The response of the two arguers was unbelievably brazen! They criticized Moshe for his previous day's action—killing an Egyptian to protect a Jew. They made it clear that they had been speaking ill of him and planned to continue to do so. Moshe declared, "The matter is known."

On the surface, it seems Moshe was referring to the fact that now people knew about what he did to the Egyptian. Yet there is something deeper here. Moshe was referring to the fact that the Jews had not yet been redeemed. He was saying that the matter (i.e., the reason) the Jews were still enslaved was obvious—they speak ill of one another behind each other's backs, so the integrity of their private deeds is therefore not developed enough for them to be redeemed.

This insight explains why a Jew who steals in private can become a slave. While every human being is expected to behave morally, the Jew's particular mission includes being incredibly particular about private speech and actions.

The man who stole publicly did wrong. The lesson of his consequences forms another discussion.

We are now focusing on the lesson of the man who stole privately. A Jew who steals privately denies an integral aspect of his Jewishness—developing Godliness in private behavior. This is why if he becomes a slave, he is called an *eved Ivri* and not an *eved Yisraeli*. For a true Yisraeli cannot be a slave to anyone or anything but Hashem.

One who is unable to be upstanding in private is not truly free. He demonstrates that he can only control himself when threatened by social consequence. An *eved Ivri* is offered freedom in the *shemittah* (sabbatical) year. Once that seventh year arrives, he is given the opportunity to control his own private choices and allow his essence—of being a Yisraeli—to shine.

The *eved Ivri* will continue to be offered the opportunity for freedom every *shemittah* year until the *yovel* (jubilee, the fiftieth) year. At that time, he is forced to be free. *Yovel* represents everything returning to its source. Ready or not, at an appointed time, each of us will return to our Source.

Hashem gives us opportunities to make efforts in the right direction without force. Each time we recognize and seize an opportunity to return to the Source, we are removing a layer of enslavement that seems to suffocate our essence. In the end, though, our essence will be revealed, and we will be faced with these questions:

- Did we *en*courage or *dis*courage the revelation process?
- Did we toil in private to be free, or did we merely await salvation?

When you are as particular in your private life as you are in public, you grow toward essential integrity. And unlike the *eved Ivri*, who continues to choose slavery until the *yovel* year, when your true essence is revealed, you will be prepared to recognize and embrace it.

You will not be surprised by its appearance, only joyfully overwhelmed by the extent of its glory.

Owning the Offering

TERUMAH

Parashat Terumah follows Parashat Mishpatim:

- First come the legalities. Then come laws of giving.
- First we must legally earn our finances. Then we share.

The letters of the Hebrew word *terumah* are the same as the letters of the word *ha'mutar*, meaning "that which is permitted." This is a way to remember that the mitzvah of *tzedakah* can only be done with that which has been acquired in a permitted manner.

I was thinking...

Money is not the only vehicle for *tzedakah*. Our actions are also charitable, and they need to be "legal" when we donate them. If I am considerate toward others in organizing a function to benefit the community, I am giving charity through "legal" means.

Before I give, I need to remind myself that *mishpatim* come first.

Literally, the word *terumah* means "raised offering." The Jewish People needed to take from their personal resources and raise those resources by offering them up to be used in the *Mishkan*, the portable Tabernacle.

Our time, energy, speech, and actions become legally our own when we "acquire" them.

How do we pay for those valuables? With humility and appreciation.

Then those commodities are ours enough to raise as offerings in the service of God, with consideration to others.

Elevated Living

TETZAVEH

In Too Soon Old, *Too Late Smart*, Gordon Livingstone writes: "We live in a society that has elevated complaint to a primary form of public discourse." We'd rather complain than examine our lives and take responsibility. One popular form of complaint is the one in which we "just missed the boat."

- "I almost had that position."
- "Her job could have/should have been mine."

In this way, we hope to elevate ourselves in the eyes of others without actually working on ourselves. Rabbi Chaim Shmuelevitz tells of a sanitation worker who once hopped off the back of a garbage truck to point out to Rav Chaim that although he was the one handling the rubbish, he could have/should have been the driver. No matter their position, people want to be thought of as more than they are.

In *Parashat Tetzaveh*, Moshe is commanded to dress his brother, Aharon, and Aharon's sons in their priestly garments. Moshe Rabbeinu is the leader of the entire nation, the greatest prophet to walk the face of the earth! Moshe Rabbeinu could have/should have been the first Kohen Gadol (High Priest). Yet he does not complain. He doesn't say, "You know, the *kehunah* (priesthood) should really have been mine."

Moshe dresses the Kohanim, and according to our Sages, Moshe deliberately chose this *parashah* to not include his name. When Hashem threatened to destroy the Jewish People after the sin of the golden calf, Moshe's words were, "*Mecheini na mi'sifrecha*—Erase me from Your Book."[1]

Rabbi Ovadia Yosef explains that the word, "*mi'sifrecha*—from Your Book," can be split to read *mi'sefer* and then the letter *chaf*, which has the numerical value of twenty. It can therefore be read as, "Erase me from the twentieth book."

Parashat Tetzaveh is the twentieth *parashah*. In other words, erase me from the *parashah* that concerns my brother's honor. Let the honor be his. Completely. No complaints. No "could have/should have."

Just responsible, elevated living, exemplified.

---

1   *Shemot* 32:32.

Assassination and Reward

KI TISA

Chur is killed. Assassinated, really, by an angry mob.

Chur was Miriam's son. He and Aharon were appointed interim leaders as Moshe ascended Har Sinai. Forty days passed, according to the nation's calculations, and the people were afraid that Moshe would never return. They demanded from Aharon and Chur a mediator in place of Moshe.

The midrash tells us that Chur rebuked the people strongly. He told them that they deserved to be beheaded for such a request! He told them they were being ungrateful for all the miracles Hashem had performed for them.

Then something crazy happened. These people, who had just experienced God's presence, who had just heard God's voice, who unequivocally knew and believed in the Almighty...hurled stones at Chur until he died! Whoa.

The situation is complex:

- The *Zohar* tells us that Hashem let Chur die this way because of the harsh words he hurled at the people.
- *Midrash Rabbah* tells us that Hashem rewarded Chur for sanctifying God's name. His grandson Betzalel would be the constructor of the Mishkan.

So,

- Was Chur right in rebuking the people? Or was he wrong?
- Did Chur die *al kiddush Hashem* (sanctifying God's name), or did he die as punishment for his harsh words?
- How can we reconcile the two explanations of Chur's death?

Chur sanctified God's name by clearly expressing unadulterated truth with no concern for his own safety. There is merit in such expression, and this may shed light on *Midrash Rabbah*'s explanation: Chur was rewarded through a grandson who would build a place for God to "reside," a place of worship according to God's instructions. This testified for all time that Chur was right in standing against the people when they were planning to worship in a prohibited manner.

So why did Chur need to die? While we cannot know God's complete accounting for one person's death, we can take a lesson. The nature of man is to fight fire with fire. When people are emotionally charged, shouting at them about how wrong and ungrateful they are may indeed be truthful, but it yields no immediate beneficial results. When a person is overwhelmed with fear, he needs to feel heard before he can examine his deeds. In other words, a person needs to feel a level of security before he/she can accept criticism. Chur offered no security and did not display sensitivity to the people's position. The people felt threatened by his harsh rebuke, and Hashem allowed human nature to run its course.

The point is that Chur's *words* were correct, but the people were not in a place to hear those words, with that tone, at that time. They were afraid and anxious. Chur's tone served to reinforce their insecurities.

> When a person is overwhelmed with fear, he needs to feel heard before he can examine his deeds.

Our intentions can be pure, and our words truthful, and we can be credited by God for those. At the same time, if we do not consider the insecurities of our audience, not only will our message go unheeded, but we will become a target for derision or worse.

To further reconcile the different explanations, Chur's punishment and reward both fit his response. His response was pure justice, with no mercy. This world cannot hold unfiltered justice—consequently, Chur left this world.

And his reward: a grandson who would achieve greatness after the grandfather had passed. Chur didn't even get to *shep nachas*. Such is the reward for a man who was not about this lifetime but about that which is timeless.

Interestingly, the word *chur* is found twice in *Megillat Esther*. *Chur* is translated as a "white material." White represents perfection, clarity. It is other-worldly and best received in this world when presented as part of an array of shades of color.

The man, Chur, deserved out-of-this-world reward for his expression of absolute truth. And he deserved a laws-of-nature punishment for not filtering that truth in the way it could be utilized in the prevailing natural conditions.

Reward and punishment respectively. Or simply consequences, as laid out by Hashem—the One Source of ultimate justice.

Contradiction reconciled.

But First, a Hamantasch

KI TISA

I have often wondered what God was thinking when He decided to make us celebrate a *chametz* (leaven)-filled holiday, Purim, just four weeks before He wants our homes to be *chametz*-free!

This can be a most frustrating expectation for the typical Jewish woman, especially as we are meant to begin preparing for each festival one month before that festival.

This week, I discovered an explanation: "You shall not make molten gods for yourself. You shall keep the Festival of Matzot."[1]

Interesting juxtaposition.

To connect these seemingly unrelated verses, *Shearit Yaakov* looks into Gemara *Megillah*: Why did the Jews deserve the threat of annihilation during the time of Mordechai and Esther? Because they served other

---

1   *Shemot* 34:17–18.

gods. The Gemara later relates that before Esther risked her life by approaching the king uninvited, Mordechai decreed that the Jews fast.

This would have been a reasonable decree…except for the fact that it was Pesach! Fast on Pesach? Mordechai's rationale was: We must repent, even if it means not celebrating Pesach, because without our repentance, the Jewish People will not live to see another Pesach! The *Shearit Yaakov* concludes that when we are careful not to serve other gods, we won't need to violate the joy of Pesach.

So, I ask, what does idol worship have to do with Pesach? *Chag Hamatzot*, "the Festival of Matzot," is about celebrating the freedom to serve God. If we are serving anything other than God, we miss out on the true joy of Pesach. The *Shearit Yaakov*'s explanation of the juxtaposition of the verses shed light for me where all was dark. Now I get it: Purim actually prepares us for Pesach!

On Purim we celebrate our drive to repent for worshipping anything less than Hashem. Anxiety, fear, worry, anger, sadness, and other unhelpful states of being can become so ingrained in our psyche that they become like molten images—sacred in their existence, appeased by our daily offerings of immobility and blaming.

- We can stop making "molten images" out of our baggage.
- We can celebrate the timing of Purim as a reminder to return and accept Hashem as the only true God.

And it is *davkah* when I feel anxious about all that *chametz* in my house just one month before Pesach that I need to not make my "stuff" into a god. It is at that time that I have the great opportunity to dump a pail of water over anything less than Hashem that I have been paying homage to. I can then gather all the ammunition (cleaning supplies) and get to scrubbing away the obstacles on the road to experiencing joy on Pesach and the taste of unleavened bread and the meaning it carries for my freedom.

Avoiding Arson

VAYAKHEL

Sarah wanted a good caterer for her parents' fiftieth anniversary. She found an ad for Jack's Kosher Catering in the classified section of the local Jewish paper. Sarah called Jack, who sounded patient and courteous. He gave Sarah contact details of references, and she called two references, who both gave glowing reports. Plus, the price seemed relatively inexpensive.

Sarah called her sister to inform her of the decision to go with Jack's catering.

"Jack?" Her sister questioned. "Jack Yates? Oh no, Sarah! Jack's no good!

"Did you know he catered for the Schwartz *brit* and burned the food? My friend Donna was there, and she told me she was appalled that a caterer would serve burnt food! Debbie was there as well. And she said only the cheese pastries were edible."

While Sarah was particular to judge others with favor, she had a hard time imagining an excuse for a caterer to serve burnt food. If her sister was right, she did not want to take the chance on their parents' anniversary party.

Sarah was about to restart her search, when a thought came to her.
Why not go to a source?

Sarah called the Schwartzes. Mrs. Schwartz answered.

"Would you recommend Jack Yates as a caterer?" she asked.

"Oh absolutely! Jack was so pleasant to work with!" Mrs. Schwartz replied.

"But, I heard he burned the food!"

Silence.

And then...

"Oy vey! Is that what you heard? I'm so glad you called me! What a terrible misunderstanding!"

Mrs. Schwartz then went on to explain that when she had asked Jack to cater for them, he had declined, saying he had another function and he liked to be present at a function he was catering. After much pleading from her, Jack finally, reluctantly, agreed to send prepared food. The family would warm up the food on the day.

Mrs. Schwartz concluded by saying, "I never dreamed that people would blame the caterer for our mistake!"

"You shall light no fire throughout your living quarters on the Shabbat day."[1] The *Shelah HaKadosh*, a sixteenth-century scholar, explains this verse. Besides the law against kindling an actual fire on Shabbat, he says we must be careful not to kindle fires of hurtful gossip on Shabbat. The gathering of family and friends on Shabbat presents more opportunity than usual to either gossip frivolously or to warm each other with our words.

If we set the flame on low before Shabbat, meaning, we are particular during the week to bring warmth to others with our words, then on Shabbat, rather than lighting fires of burning gossip, we'll be dishing out warm compliments.

(Story adapted from *The Other Side of the Story* by Yehudis Samet.)

---

1   *Shemot* 35:3.

Give Strong

VAYAKHEL

Years ago, when we were living in the Holy Land, I would regularly take my little boys to the *gan ha'ir*, the local playground. On one occasion, there were three little girls playing "house" on the platform atop the slide. The tallest one announced "*Ani ima!* (I'm the mommy!)" The other two happily became the baby and the sister.

Then something fascinating happened. The *ima* plopped herself down, and with a great sigh, she cried out, "*Oy! Ein li ko'ach!* (I have no strength!)" One girl tried to get the "mommy" to accompany her down the slide. And the "mommy" kept repeating, "*Ein li ko'ach! Ein li ko'ach!*" She could not even muster the strength to give her "daughter" a little joy by pushing herself enough to ride the slide and land at the bottom. That "mommy" could give nothing.

Just then, I made a decision (as I ran to stop my middle child from throwing sand at his older brother). I decided not just to have strength to give—I also wanted my giving to be strong! I knew I would only be able to maintain strong giving if I would regularly self-administer the appropriate amount of fuel made available by the Source of all. I would tap into available resources, including sleep, healthy eating habits, good people, positive thoughts, prayer, music, enjoyable activities. I knew if I would fuel myself, I could give strong.

In *Parashat Vayakhel*, we learn about giving. "*Kol nediv libo*—Whoever is of a willing heart shall bring as gifts to Hashem."[1] And later, the proclamation, "The Jewish People brought *nedavah* to Hashem."[2]

Nediv is when the heart motivates the body—I feel, therefore I give. Interestingly, the word *nediv* can be found throughout *Tanach* relating to noblemen or princes, as in "*nedivei ha'am*,"[3] referring to Moshe and Aharon; and in *Tehillim*, "*Mi'betoach b'nedivim*"[4] and "*Al tivtechu b'nedivim*,"[5] reminding us to rely on Hashem rather than noblemen. There are many more times we find the word *nediv* referring to nobles in *Tehillim*, as well as in *Mishlei, Shir Hashirim, Iyov,* and *Yeshayahu*. The same root word that refers to internal motivation also means nobility.

On the surface, the two understandings could not reflect more different meanings. When a person behaves nobly, we think of them as acting without personal interest. So how can one word imply both "driven by the self" and at the same time "driven by something beyond the self"?

The answer lies in the definition of self.

There is a beautiful *tefillah* (prayer) hanging on my kitchen cabinet door. It is attributed to Rabbi Aryeh Kaplan, and includes these lines: "Oh God, help us to find that point of light within us. Help us to make it grow into a bright flame, so that it may consume all the pain, all the confusion, all the emptiness that is in our hearts. Help us to find You, oh God. For as we find You, even so, shall we find ourselves."

At our innermost core, the source of our life is our *neshamah*, our untainted connection to Hashem. All of our human drives, thoughts, and

---

1   *Shemot* 35:5.
2   Ibid., 35:29.
3   *Bamidbar* 21:18.
4   *Tehillim* 118:9.
5   Ibid., 146:3.

organs with their systems can easily deflect attention away from the line of connection. Reaching that line of connection, that innermost core, is actually how I reach beyond my self. Therefore, when a person is *nediv lev*, he is being driven by the innermost self, which is connected to that which is most nobly beyond the self.

I wonder if the *nesi'im* (princes) might have been listed in the Torah as *nedivim* had they given immediately to the *Mishkan*. Earlier, in their desire to be exclusive, they missed out on an opportunity to be *nedivim*. They allowed their "middle" selves—their logic and ego—to get in the way of their core and higher selves. True *nedavah* is when a person gives because their heart is moved to be closer to Hashem. On a practical note, let's not fool ourselves into thinking it is possible to give everyone what they want and need all the time. Still, if we make the conscious decision to do so, we will find that we can fuel ourselves into providing wholehearted, sustained giving much of the time.

In the haftarah corresponding to this reading, we read about King Shlomo building the First Beit Hamikdash (Temple). There were two ornate pillars at the entrance of the Beit Hamikdash, and they were called "Yachin" and "Boaz."[6]

Our Sages teach us that in the battle with the *yetzer hara*—the urge to disconnect from God—there must be *yachin*, "preparation," if we hope to have *boaz*, "strength in it." If we think we stand a chance at overcoming the *yetzer hara* without preparing daily, we have another thing coming. We must continually prepare ourselves and care for ourselves in a way that renews our strength so we may give of ourselves in service of our Sustainer.

In *Tehillim* 113, we sing, "*Mekimi mei'afar dal*—He raises the lowly from dust, *l'hoshivi im nedivim*—to seat them with *nedivim*." *L'hoshivi* means "to seat them," and it also means "to return them." So it's not that Hashem simply saves me from lowliness when I am depleted—Hashem reinstates me. He continually returns me to where I belong inside myself, so I can yearn for and reach a higher vantage point, which is

---

6   *Melachim I* 7:21.

beyond the self. And from there, I can give and keep fueling myself with His provisions.

And although I'll often land at the bottom, in the dust, from there I know I will rise again with energy to give and declare, "*Yesh li ko'ach!* (I have strength!)"

What Is Done

PEKUDEI

When I met the man who would become my husband, I was an observant sixteen-year-old chapter president of the local youth group, NCSY, and he was a cool nineteen-year-old guitar-playing advisor.

Shabbatons were staple events for NCSY throughout the year. There were four musical spaces in each Shabbaton that made it "classic NCSY." The last was "closing," the Sunday-morning farewell.

In California, my not-yet-husband, besides being advisor for two city chapters, was also the program coordinator for the West Coast region. Plus, he was the band. On Sunday mornings, with hundreds of "sad-it's-over" teenagers swaying arm in arm, he would strum the familiar tune of *"Lo Alecha Hamelachah Ligmor."* The words are from *Pirkei Avot*: "It is not on you to complete the work. And you are not free to be excused from it."[1]

Emotions were high (as they are in teenagers, especially tired ones), and the message of these parting words would be a source of comfort

---

1   *Pirkei Avot* 2:16.

and motivation as the kids headed back to their uninspiring, mostly secular lives.

In *Parashat Pekudei*, Hashem tells us, "And they brought the *Mishkan* to Moshe."[2] This wording seems strange, as Moshe was the one who actually assembled the *Mishkan*. The people did not bring the *Mishkan*; they brought the accessories—the clasps and beams, the pillars and curtains, utensils and spices, etc.

The midrash connects this verse to a story about Rabbi Abahu, who was known for influencing the royal court in favor of his fellow Jews. Once, Rabbi Abahu was shown a vision of his great reward in the World to Come. He replied joyfully, "All this is prepared for me, and here I thought I had worked in vain!"

What was Rabbi Abahu saying? Did he not have faith that Hashem would reward him for his goodness? Rabbi Abahu had faith, but his joy in seeing a vision of what lay in store for him stemmed from the new clarity that he would be rewarded as if he had succeeded, even regarding attempts that did not manifest in observable success.

Flashback to the Jews in the desert: After the Jewish People had collected and worked to create all that was needed for the *Mishkan*, some may have been disappointed that they would not get to actually erect the structure; they would not get to finish what they had started. The wording of the verse, "And they brought the *Mishkan* to Moshe," tells us that their contribution was considered a finished product.

In Boston, Rabbi Miller (by then my husband) would run workshops for parents of teenagers. He would open with this statement: "We cannot control the end result, but we can offer our children the structure and tools they can use to become responsible adults."

One mother was particularly agitated by this idea. "Well, what's the point of being a good parent if it won't guarantee me a good child?"

We, like this mother, will forever feel frustrated until we understand that "it is not on you to finish the work. And you are not free to be excused from it."

---

2   *Shemot* 39:33.

For what are we held accountable? For the time, effort, and energy we put into establishing goodness!

- This was the message for the disappointed *Mishkan* contributors.
- This was the message for the concerned Rabbi Abahu.
- This was the message sung to those saddened teens at "closing."

We need to take this message in the forms available to us. Be it Torah study. Or workshops. Or even as a catchy tune performed by a cool, guitar-playing nineteen-year-old.

VAYIKRA

So Close

VAYIKRA

A sacrifice is a giving up of something that brings us comfort, pleasure, or security. Why sacrifice?

A friend had been married a few months and was unhappy. She felt sad, angry, unsupported, unappreciated, and tired. When she confided in a mentor, who established that her husband was a good guy and that her daily schedule was crazy busy, the mentor suggested that part of the problem lay with the new bride.

"You've not given up anything from your previous existence to accommodate your new reality," the mentor challenged. "You're working like you're single, expecting the benefits of being married. The problem is…you're not sacrificing."

In Hebrew, the word for a sacrifice that was brought in the Beit Hamikdash is *korban*.

The root of *korban* is *karov*, "close." *Parashat Vayikra* focuses on the laws of sacrifices. Bringing a sacrifice was a way to come close to God:

- When you sacrifice for the relationship, the consequence is closeness.
- No sacrifice—no closeness.

When we deem closeness as more important than the security of past routine, we are ready to bring a *korban*. When the newlywed cut an hour out of her workday, and she used that time to invest in self-care with the intention of bringing more of her whole self into her marriage, her bitterness dissipated. "It's like giving a dollar and, in time, receiving a hundred million dollars," she said.

Before the hundred million can appear, though, we must have enough faith in the relationship—and enough desire to be closer—to let go of that one dollar.

Fault Lines

VAYIKRA

I called Telkom, the South African telephone company, and I got this recording: "Dear Customer, thank you for using our online fault reporting solution. Your fault has been logged on to a telephone number and a reference number. Please refer to your fault reference number in all correspondence with Telkom in this regard. Alternatively, you can track your fault progress online. Kind regards, Telkom"

So. They've identified what's my fault. And they've logged my fault into their system. And they want me to refer to my fault whenever I communicate with them. Also, I can go online to see just how much is my fault!

Great.

In *Parashat Vayikra*, verses 22–23 read: "If/When a ruler sins...he will bring an offering."

Here, the word *asher* is used to indicate "if" or "when." This is an unusual word to use for this meaning. *Asher* is usually translated as "which." This poses a grammatical difficulty, *which* we are willing to let slide—once we gain perspective.

Asher is the same root as *ashrei*, "fortunate." Is there something fortunate about a leader bringing a sin offering? Yes. A leader who brings a sin offering is a leader who recognizes his mistakes.

Rav Moshe Feinstein expounds: There is no complete perfection in this world. While we may be inclined to think that our leaders should never make mistakes, that is unrealistic. The fact that the Torah tells us specifically what type of sin offering the leader will bring means that the leader will transgress! And since a faultless leader does not exist, better a leader who recognizes his faults than one who does not.

Building on this, Rav Moshe offers practical advice on decision-making. When faced with a choice, we must not wait to find a perfect choice. Rather, we should choose the one with the least disadvantages. If we expect perfection, we set ourselves up for chronic indecision. After all, only God is perfect, and only God is ideal. When we accept this reality, we'll find decision-making easier.

And the side effects? We will be less disappointed. Less frustrated. More forgiving. Instead of thinking, *Fortunate are those with perfect leaders, lives, children, jobs…*

We can shift our perspective:

- Fortunate are those with leaders who recognize their mistakes.
- Fortunate are those with friends and relatives who recognize their imperfections.
- Fortunate are those who recognize their own faults.
- Fortunate are those who do not await the perfect choice.

Which brings us to appreciate Telkom service and the reminder to check our own fault progress. With kind regards, of course.

Remember Shabbat

TZAV

I once overheard my six- and eight-year-old playing an absurd game of "Opposites." This was the exchange:

"What's the opposite of couch?"

"Umm...book?"

"No. What's the opposite of forest?"

"Umm...box?"

"No. What's the opposite of dancer?"

"Um...no dancer?"

"Yes. Your turn."

That exchange came to mind when I learned this from *Pirkei D'Rabi Eliezer*: "Amalek is the opposite of Shabbat."

What does that mean? Haman, in the Purim story, was a descendant of Amalek, and we have a mitzvah to destroy the nation of Amalek. Why? Because God said so.

Still, when we want to understand Hashem's commandments for the purpose of growing closer to Him, we delve in...

Historically, Amalek's behavior has shown that they are bothered by the fact that we are the moral and spiritual soul of the world. Okay. The Babylonians, Persians, Greeks, and Romans were bothered by the same. As bad as they were, they weren't Amalek. How is Amalek different?

While all those nations, including Amalek, wanted to disconnect us from our Source, Amalek also wants to annihilate us. Let's see how each nation treated us:

- Under Babylonian rule, we were exiled from Israel, and the Beit Hamikdash was destroyed.
- The Persians invited us to wild parties.
- The Greeks demanded Hellenism or death.
- The Romans killed Torah-learners and mitzvah-observers. Then they destroyed the Second Beit Hamikdash.
- Later enemies demanded conversion or death.

Amalek is different. Amalek says, "We're not cutting any deals with you. We're not asking you to renounce your beliefs. We're not out to destroy your places of worship. We just want you dead."

While Amalek is our greatest enemy, they remind us most of who we are. No matter if I deny core Jewish beliefs. No matter if I run away from home. I can kick and scream at my brothers, "You're not my people!" Still, if I was born into Judaism or converted to it, there is no getting out of the family. Ever.

So how is Amalek the opposite of Shabbat? The *Shem MiShmuel* teaches that each of the two times we are commanded to keep Shabbat, we are given different reasons.

- First: We keep Shabbat to show that Hashem created the world and imbued it with holiness.
- Second: We remember the way Hashem took us out of Egypt by using the physical world in service of Him.

Our enemies do not want us to keep Shabbat. They do not want there to be a display of Godliness in the world because Godliness undermines their desire to be seen as all-powerful. They are satisfied that they have fulfilled their mission of "owning us" when they can cause us to break that bond with God. Yet they all leave out the crucial second purpose of Shabbat—except Amalek, who knows better. Amalek knows that Shabbat is not just about declaring God the Creator, Sustainer, and Imbuer of Holiness. Amalek knows that Shabbat is also about potential in the physical world, and that there is power in physical existence. Amalek knows that as long as one Jew lives, there is an opportunity for Godliness to blossom.

Every year on the Shabbat before Purim, we read *Parashat Zachor*, which means "Chapter of Remembrance." We read: "Remember what Amalek did to you when you left Egypt," and yet, we have a mitzvah to blot out the memory of Amalek.

Do we remember? Or do we not remember? Simply, we need to remember what they did, yet leave no trace of their existence. The best way to destroy evidence is to consume it, to digest it.

> Amalek knows that as long as one Jew lives, there is an opportunity for Godliness to blossom.

Let's digest this. "Amalek is the opposite of Shabbat."

Yes, Shabbat is holy, and we try to tap into that, and we add special prayers and blessings. At the same time, let's realize what Amalek has known for centuries: It is only through our physicality that we properly observe Shabbat. Our physical existence is the basis of our holiness, so the only way to completely annihilate Shabbat is to annihilate us!

It's so ridiculously clear! How could our other enemies not pick up on this? How could they think that by forcing us to "convert" they'd be rid of our spiritual influence?

I'd like to suggest that our other enemies actually believed in the power of their gods, and actually thought that their beliefs were true. Since they were wrong, they were not the ultimate threat. Amalek is the ultimate threat because he knows the dual meaning of Shabbat—that Hashem is the Source of all *and* that it is through our physical existence that we can bring this recognition to the world.

On the surface, Amalek is on a mission to destroy us. With the deeper understanding that there is no force separate from Hashem, Amalek is simultaneously on another mission: to remind us of our crucial role in the world. When we have clarity in this, Amalek is no longer a necessary part of God's plan. He is made redundant and disappears without a trace.

What's the opposite of Amalek?

Umm…no Amalek?

Yes!

And Shabbat.

When Celebrating Equals Mourning

SHEMINI

We celebrate Purim. Yet there is so much suffering in the world. How can we dance and sing and make merry while there is so much loss and death in the world that others are immediately experiencing?

The *parashah* opens, "And it was on the eighth day." Moshe had told his brother, Aharon the Kohen Gadol, that as part of his priestly inauguration process, he was not to leave the Tent of Meeting for seven days. These were exciting days for Aharon as he prepared himself to further fulfill his life's calling. Yet the *Midrash Tanchuma* tells us something else: Moshe's intent was for the seven days to serve as days that Aharon would sit shivah for his sons.

News flash: Aharon's sons had not yet passed away! So what is the meaning of this midrash?

Rabbi Mordechai Gifter offers an enlightening insight. The purpose of the seven-day mourning period is not just to express sorrow. It is a time to reflect and conclude that everything, even suffering and death, stems from God. The seven days that Aharon blissfully spent in the Tent of Meeting brought him to an elevated state. It was in this state that he received the news of his sons' deaths. And it was in this state that Aharon was silent and accepting of that fate.

Rav Gifter says that the seven days preceding his sons' deaths accomplished the same as seven days of mourning. As much as we may be able to intellectually grasp this idea, the practicality of it can seem too foreign for us to hold. So we need to bring it home.

Yes, there is pain and loss. There is also pleasure and gain. On Purim, and any day, if we dance to hide God, we will spiral into a deeper sense of loss, for there is no loss greater than losing God. But if we allow God into our dancing, we climb up to a greater sense of connectedness, for there is no gain greater than finding God.

On Wanting

TAZRIA

The five-year-old wants a bike. The nine-year-old wants an iPod. The thirteen-year-old wants a new sweatshirt (that looks old)... a smartphone, a later curfew, her own room.

I say...let them want!

If we think that the feeling of wanting is bad, we'll do whatever we can to avoid that yearning. We'll either procure what we want as quickly as we can, or we'll deny that the yearning exists.

Torah law prohibits physical contact between man and wife while the woman is considered *niddah*, until she counts the appropriate number of days and immerses in a mikvah. The laws of *taharat ha'mishpachah* create an opportunity for yearning within the marriage. Isn't it amazing? God wants us to yearn.

In *Parashat Tazria*, a woman who has just given birth is instructed to wait after childbirth until she may enter the Beit Hamikdash and bring a sacrifice. With the understanding that now a void exists where a life resided, the new mother is given time—in which yearning can fill that void.

At the Pesach Seder, in the haggadah, we read that the people cried out to Hashem. Then the verse reads: "And He heard our cries, saw our affliction, our burden, and our oppression."[1] We can wonder, *Hashem only heard our cries now? Where was Hashem all the years before?* This crying out is 209 years from the time the original seventy Jews entered Egypt. Granted, the oppression was not immediate. Still, what took Hashem so long to hear the cries of the people?

Rabbi Yochanan Zweig explains: The Jews tolerated the slow turn from tax-paying civilians, to patriotic workers for the Egyptian economy, to heavily taxed, overworked, unpaid, and then beaten laborers. Certainly, they groaned and complained among themselves. Certainly, there was sadness and tears. Still, for years they simply lived with the inconvenience, discomfort, and then the pain of slavery. Until Pharaoh began to kill the children. Then the people let themselves yearn for freedom, and they cried out. Not only did they cry out, but they put an address on their cries—they cried out to Hashem!

The Jews finally allowed themselves to feel their deepest yearning—to survive as a nation. It seems that Hashem had been waiting for the Jews to let themselves feel that yearning. He had been waiting for them to show desire for the next stage. When they finally reached a great, desperate yearning that overflowed beyond self-pity—and they channeled their yearning to the Source of survival—then Hashem allowed Himself to "hear" and "see" that the Jews were ready for more than just sympathy. They were ready for redemption to begin.

Yearning is good:

- We are enjoined to yearn each day for Mashiach to arrive.
- We are meant to long for the time when peace and clarity will prevail.
- In *Birkat Hamazon* and daily prayers we say that we want Yerushalayim to be rebuilt.

This is not lip service to some unattainable paradise. Two Batei Mikdash have been destroyed. After the destruction of the first by the

---

1   *Devarim* 26:7.

Babylonians, the Jews had only to wait seventy years for its rebuilding. Yet we have been waiting for the third and final Beit Hamikdash since the Romans razed the Second Beit Hamikdash grounds in 70 CE! Perhaps the challenge—the test we have not yet passed in this exile—is about wanting. We need to stop being afraid to want. Often, we'd rather avoid the possibility of disappointment and the discomfort of not having what we want than allow ourselves to live with deep yearning.

We need to value the yearning and see it as Hashem's way to get us to move closer to Him. Children need to be given space to want if they are to grow into adults who know how to yearn. Validating desire is a sublime way to allow for healthy acceptance and celebration of that sense called yearning. Yearning keeps us working toward Hashem as we desire to be close to Him, despite the fact that we will never fully know His being.

Allowing ourselves to want opens the door to feeling appreciation for all that does manifest, and anticipation for all that can manifest.

Long live the wanting!

We need to stop being afraid to want. Often, we'd rather avoid the possibility of disappointment and the discomfort of not having what we want than allow ourselves to live with deep yearning.

Constancy
and Renewal

TAZRIA

"Constancy" and "renewal" are two aspects of what we need in our lives. *Parashat Tazria* opens with laws of spiritual purity concerning a woman who has just given birth, and amid these laws is the mitzvah to circumcise a boy on the eighth day.

A Jew is the only being who can change his/her status from *tahor* (spiritually pure) to *tamei* (spiritually impure), and vice versa. A Jew can rise and fall in spiritual status depending on his actions and experiences.

Being involved in the great mitzvah of burying the dead results in spiritual impurity, so maintaining spiritual purity is not a goal in itself. Yet spiritual purity is a necessary prerequisite for certain actions:

- A Kohen had to be *tahor* in order to properly carry out the services in the Beit Hamikdash.
- A man's wife must be *tahor* in order to properly carry out marital relations.

Today, without a Beit Hamikdash for priestly service, it is the Jewish wife who continues the practice of affecting individual spiritual status. When I have the privilege of accompanying a bride to the mikvah, I ask Hashem to open her heart and mind to upholding the continual mitzvot of *taharat ha'mishpachah*, family spiritual purity.

While the woman has the continual reminder of the capacity for spiritual purity and impurity, the Jewish man has the *brit milah*, the covenant of circumcision, as a reminder of his capacity for *tumah* and *taharah*. Notice the difference:

- The *brit* is a constant reminder.
- A woman's sign is not constant. Hers is one of renewal.

In our lives, we need constancy *and* renewal:

- The constants keep us grounded.
- Renewal brings inspiration.
- Grounding without inspiration leads to detachment, untapped dynamics, and the possibility for the constant to lack connection to its meaning.
- Renewal without the constancy leads to unfocused search for meaning and pleasure.

Brit milah is man's opportunity for initiation into Jewish life. Once done, it is constant. *Taharat ha'mishpachah* is woman's opportunity to be inspired and carry that inspiration into her home. Once done, it is not constant. Her status will fall again. Inspiration will need to be renewed.

To continue securely on our journey through lifelong learning and growth, we need the observance of the constant mitzvot and the inspiration that renewal provides. Constancy and renewal are gatekeepers of our spousal relationships.

Each and both.

What You Are

METZORA

When I was a kid, if I or my friends were insulted, we'd chant, "Whatever you say is what you are!" Without even realizing it, we were chanting a true concept. What a person calls somebody else, he himself is.

We recently read that the *metzora* (one with the spiritual affliction that displays itself on the skin) must call out, concerning himself, "*Tamei tamei*—Impure, impure."[1] In the past, this person drew attention to the "impurities" of others. As part of his healing and atonement process, he must draw attention to his own impurity. In the Talmud there is a discussion in which we find the wording: "With his own blemish, he disqualifies others."[2] In other words, if I say, "You're lazy," I'm deflecting my laziness by looking for indolence in you.

Back to the *metzora*, healing will only follow honest self-reflection. The first step in growing out of any character-based flaw is to recognize

---

1   *Vayikra* 13:45.
2   *Kiddushin* 70b.

that flaw. We might think that for the *metzora* to see his skin afflicted is enough to change him. But no; by just seeing the affliction, the *metzora* may erroneously conclude that in order to be rid of it, he need only pray to Hashem, the Source Who brought the disease. That's not enough. In order to be rid of it, he must declare himself as the one with the problem. The *metzora* will only recover when he admits that he is responsible for identifying his own faults so that he can put forth the efforts to grow out of them.

And it occurs to me that the underlying cause of disrespecting others is a lack of proper self-esteem. For if one truly knew his own worth, he would be courageous enough to live up to that worth in deed and speech.

So "Whatever you say is what you are" is not entirely true. It's more like, "Whatever you say is what you think you are, and you only said that because you don't realize your immeasurable worth; otherwise, you would see immeasurable worth in every human being, and you would only speak with connection to that worth."

But that's not quite as catchy.

Don't Crack the Code

METZORA

> Code of Conduct
>
> Welcome to our Coffee Shop. We strive to create a culture of warmth and belonging and respectfully request that everyone abides by the following rules:
>
> - Use spaces as intended: Sleeping, smoking, consuming alcohol, drug use, or improper use of restrooms is not permitted.
> - Be considerate of others: Loud or unreasonable noise is not tolerated.
> - Communicate with respect: Obscene harassing, abusive language or gestures are unacceptable.
> - Act responsibly: Violating any law, ordinance, or regulation is prohibited.
>
> We want our store to be a place where everyone can gather and connect. Those disrupting the environment may be asked to leave.

This sign was posted on the bulletin board in a local café.

It got me thinking. In *Parashat Acharei Mot*, Aharon's sons have just died. Their death seems a consequence of their "illegal" activity. Now, to be fair, there was no sign up in the *Mishkan* to deter the men from bringing an offering in an unprescribed manner.

Such a sign might have read:

> ## Code of Conduct
>
> Welcome to the *Mishkan*. We strive to create a culture of connection to Hashem. Please abide by the following rules:
>
> - Use spaces as intended: Sleeping, smoking, drinking alcohol, or improper use of rooms is not permitted.
> - Be considerate of others: Unnecessary noise is not tolerated.
> - Act responsibly: Bringing an offering in any way other than how Hashem has prescribed is prohibited, especially if you might have done any one of the following:
>   - Rendered judgment in front of your teacher
>   - Not married, thinking no woman is good enough for you
>   - Been too casual with Hashem, looking directly at His presence at Har Sinai
>   - Tried to seize power, not asking advice from colleagues and teachers
>
> We want our *Mishkan* to be a place that will atone for the disconnect of the sin of the golden calf. Those disrupting that atonement will die.

While that's a pretty scary sign, perhaps such a sign would have been enough of a deterrent to prevent Aharon's sons, Nadav and Avihu, from bringing their offering in a manner that led to their death.

Here's the thing, though. Nadav and Avihu were not "customers" in the *Mishkan*. They were staff. They were leaders. They had just gone through an intense week-long orientation. Signs in stores are for customers, not staff. (Except the ones about handwashing in the bathrooms, which kinda worry me—if staff need to be reminded to wash their hands...) Staff have whole handbooks of expectations and consequences. There are certain behaviors that customers could be punished lightly for, i.e, they may be asked to leave. Yet those same behaviors from staff are grounds for dismissal. There is a basic respect that leaders must embody if they are to lead.

Sadly, we live in a society that has this backward: Leaders are excused when they blatantly disregard the value of individual human beings in the name of the bigger picture:

- She's too busy running the business to speak respectfully to the desk clerk.
- He's too worried about making that deal to say thank you to the waiter.

It starts with small actions of disrespect, and when those indiscretions are continually disregarded, worse infractions are certain to follow. And, inevitably, what began as basic disrespect becomes crimes and abuses.

The fact that Nadav and Avihu were not held accountable for earlier transgressions and spiraled until their behavior was out of control teaches me that this is a pattern that we can expect when people in leadership consistently get away with behavior that would never be tolerated from their clients.

So I appreciate that coffee shop sign, because it tells me that individuals will be held accountable if they do not abide by the basic code of conduct. And if there really is a follow-through, if a customer is actually asked to leave for breaking the code, that would save them from continuing down a path of lack of accountability toward a potentially devastating fate.

Let's hold ourselves accountable for small actions of disrespect, to the point that posted codes of conduct in cafés seem simultaneously no-brainers and hopeful signs that accountability matters.

Enjoy your coffee.

Miss the Mark

KEDOSHIM

Years ago, in the summer sleepaway camp where I worked, a colleague and I made the decision to send a teenage girl home. She had been cutting herself. Much as we wished we could hold her close, we knew it was the better decision to have her go home.

In *Parashat Kedoshim*, we find two prohibitions in one verse:

- "And cutting for the dead (*v'seret l'nefesh*) you shall not make in your flesh,"
- "And imprints of marking you shall not put on yourself."[1]

So:

- Cutting oneself is prohibited.
- Markings (tattoos) are prohibited.

Regarding cutting, why is the word *l'nefesh* used? Because *l'nefesh* is usually translated as "for the dead," and it refers to the way the ancient Emorites would mourn for their dead. They would cut themselves

---

1   *Vayikra* 19:28.

to express sadness over the loss of life. By prohibiting this behavior, Hashem is telling us that self-harm is not the way to cope with emotional pain.

Any prohibition, if it is to be respected, must be seen as part of a greater picture. If God says don't do it, it means do whatever you can to ensure that you don't do it! In other words, put yourself in places where your worth as a Godly being can be reinforced, and you will come to hold prohibitions as precious guidelines for maintaining a life that befits you—a life of goodness.

- By self-harming, a person pulls herself deeper into her pain until she is enveloped by it.
- On the other hand, by self-helping, a person stretches herself beyond her pain.

There is necessary discomfort in moving through the hurt, letting yourself feel that emotional pain, with the awareness that you are bigger than that pain. Self-harm is a diversion from the work of life. Hence, the cutting is *l'nefesh*, "for the dead"—for the part of oneself that is stuck.

> Put yourself in places where your worth as a Godly being can be reinforced, and you will come to hold prohibitions as precious guidelines for maintaining a life that befits you—a life of goodness.

I'll explain: To be alive includes moving courageously, responsibly, through pain, because circumstances and feelings change. Cutting begins with the thinking that circumstances will never change. "I will always be sad, bad, wrong, worthless." But "nothing will ever change" is only true concerning someone who is dead.

And this explains why the prohibition against "imprints of marking," i.e., tattooing, follows the law against cutting. Clearly, getting a tattoo is not the same as "cutting." Yet, in my mind, there is an interesting connection. Getting a tattoo is like marrying someone who insists that you never change. At first, this may sound cool, like all those love songs about wanting you just the way you are.

Suppose, though, that you want to explore new interests as you age, or you discover dormant talents. Then your spouse's insistence is no longer cool—it becomes a straitjacket that holds you in a stagnant place. It becomes difficult for you to strive for new goals and growth, to reach beyond where you were when you tied the knot...or dyed the skin. You are branded with markings that represent your mindset during a particular time.

Hashem wants us to keep growing—to keep moving through pain, experiencing pleasure in the bodies He has given us with the limitations He has placed on them. When we attach ourselves to the One who is free from all constraints, we cut ourselves loose from engaging in self-destructive behavior, and we free ourselves to be ever involved in the process of self-construction.

A Brand-New Night

EMOR

Parents, you can relate to this:

It's your child's bedtime. You have been frustrated by your child's behavior for most of the day.

Since the moment he awoke, he's been on your nerves—not moving fast enough to get himself out to school on time, making trouble in school, refusing to do homework, picking on his sister. And the list goes on. You, as a parent, have plenty of justification for sending him to bed without a goodnight cuddle or a kind word. After all, isn't it enough that you let him live today?

You think, *Tomorrow, if he behaves well, he'll get some bedtime cuddles. I don't like him enough right now to offer that.* So you tell him to get to bed. You say, "I hope you'll think about how you behaved today and make tomorrow better." You say this without looking at him.

In *Parashat Emor* we find the following verse, which relates to when a Kohen serving in the Beit Hamikdash can eat from his offerings if he has been *tamei*: "And when the sun is down, he shall be spiritually pure

140

(*tahor*) and afterward he may eat from holy things."[1] At nightfall, all priests can partake in the meat from the daily offerings.

In his *sefer, Wellsprings of Torah*, Alexander Zusia Friedman points out a Mishnah in *Berachot* that relates to Kohanim waiting till nightfall if they had been *tamei* in the daytime: "When is the *Shema* to be read in the evening service? When the priests go in to eat their offering."

This halachah tells us that our daytime acceptance that "Hashem is our God, Hashem is one" lasts only as long as daylight. Nightfall brings a new era that necessitates renewed acceptance of God's reality.

This Mishnah is teaching about when to say the *Shema*. Why doesn't the Mishnah simply state, "Say *Shema* after nightfall"? By using a Kohen's spiritual status in connection with the nighttime *Shema*, the authors of the Mishnah invite us to draw connections.

Here's one: Don't rest on your laurels of the day to carry you through the night. Rather, nightly, renew your commitment to building on those laurels.

Here's another: Don't let the deficiencies of the day hold you back from maximizing the unique opportunities of night. Nighttime is a new time. Just because we spent the day in one space doesn't mean our nighttime must continue in that space.

Back to that child and a parent's frustration. Nighttime is a new era. I need not wait till morning to see my child as deserving of acceptance. God purposely created time and its natural transitions. These natural breaks are opportunities for us humans to slow down, stop, evaluate, recommit, recharge, or change course. And parents have an added opportunity to teach their children how to optimize God-given transition times.

God Himself does this by offering opportunities to connect to Godliness at different times. "Now it's night," God says to the priest. "Enjoy the offering, because now is a new era."

We say to ourselves, "Hashem is our God, Hashem is One," because we want to renew the potency of our daytime declaration. A parent says to

---

1   *Vayikra* 22:7.

a child, "I love you. And I am blessed to be your parent," because a child should not go to bed thinking that his parent's love no longer applies or that the potency of parental commitment will expire.

Just Us

BEHAR

The great sage, Hillel HaZakein, was walking down the road. He met a group of merchants selling wheat.

"How much for a *se'ah* [a measurement]?" he asked.

"Two coins," they responded.

Later, Hillel met another group of merchants, who told him that they were selling the same amount of wheat for three coins. Hillel asked why their wheat was more expensive than the other merchants' wheat.

"You stupid Babylonian!" the second merchants said with derision. "Don't you know that the price of grain depends on the amount of labor invested in the process?"

The story could end with Hillel, in his inimitable style, not responding and just humbly moving on. After all, anyone who calls Hillel (or anyone) "stupid" is clearly lacking in *middot tovot* (good character traits). And Hillel HaZakein was known for his patience and understanding.

Yet the story continues, and Hillel rebukes the merchants: "I asked you a valid question. Why do you insult me?"

The merchants realize they transgressed the mitzvah of "a man shall not cause pain to his fellow." Then they do *teshuvah*.

The mitzvah of *ona'at devarim*, not causing pain with words, is found in *Parashat Emor*,[1] following the mitzvah not to upset others in business dealings: "If you sell or buy anything from another Jew, do not cause pain to him."[2] This is understood as a directive to salesmen: Do business justly.

Interesting that for both commandments the word for "do harm" is the same—*tonu*. In interpersonal relationships, as in business dealings, we have harmed each other if we have not dealt justly. Perhaps this explains why Hillel did not remain silent in the above vignette. Had the merchants merely insulted Hillel with no valid explanation for their higher price, Hillel probably would have remained silent. By stating a logical reason for selling more expensive grain, it seems they understood the idea of being fair in business. If they could grasp the idea of being righteous in business, maybe they could grasp the idea of righteousness in communication as well.

I am blown away by Hillel HaZakein! Rather than focusing on any sense of personal insult, Hillel was focused on what he could do for others. Here, he had a chance to help these men fulfill a mitzvah. And so he did—without anger, without shaming, and with businessman logic, as businessmen need. We would do well to learn from Hillel and respond to others by considering what they can hear; to not melt, retaliate, or grow arrogant in the face of insult; to recognize that each person owns his words as each person owns his deeds; and to see the world as a place of opportunity to learn and to give.

There is so much negativity in life. How I react to it depends on me. If I don't think much of myself, I will focus on what hurts me. I will actually await the insults and be able to find them in almost every interaction!

A better way to live is like Hillel HaZakein, who said, "*Im ani kan ha'kol kan*—If I am here, everything/everyone is here." If I am in this situation, I have all I need to actualize the potential of this moment, in this

---

1   *Vayikra* 25:17.
2   Ibid., 25:14.

space. Hillel knew that anyone who called him "stupid" was the same as anyone who called anyone stupid. We are each "anyone," and we are each "everyone."

And with that in mind, we have plenty of business to take care of. Justly and without harm.

A Case for Study

BECHUKOTAI

Anti–Semitism is a threat to Jewish life, and so is assimilation.

Parashat Bechukotai opens with a list of blessings we will enjoy when we live up to Hashem's expectations of us. Then the *parashah* lists terrifying consequences that will befall us if we disregard those expectations, if we assimilate. How does a Jew assimilate? How do so many Jews assimilate?

Rashi (the renowned medieval French commentator) lists seven steps of alienation from Jewish heritage. It is understood that these steps may be taken over years and may span generations. In other words, a child may be born to parents who are already three or four steps into alienation. At the same time, one individual could walk herself all seven steps away from Judaism.

The steps to "walk away" from Judaism are:

1. Failure to study diligently/regularly
2. Failure to keep mitzvot

3. Despising Torah-observant Jews
4. Hating Torah scholars (Rabbi Akiva, who was arguably the greatest Torah scholar in history, was on this level before he returned.)
5. Preventing other Jews from observing the Torah
6. Denial that mitzvot are God-given
7. Denial of God's existence and active providence

As the Jewish People assimilate, they open themselves to the consequences mentioned in the *parashah*. Still, we are assured that when we desire to affiliate with the unassimilated, Hashem brings the blessings back. How do we display this desire? Well, how did Rabbi Akiva display the desire to return from assimilation? Rabbi Akiva's first step was to learn: He learned the Hebrew alphabet, then *Tanach* (Written Torah), and, later, he would plumb the depths of the Talmud (Oral Torah).

One may have thought that to bring himself back from assimilation, Rabbi Akiva would backtrack in the order that he fell away from Judaism—first working on loving Torah scholars and observant Jews, then keeping mitzvot, and eventually getting around to learning—yet, we see that he got straight to the learning.

I am not suggesting that we should not work on loving others and performing mitzvot. I am saying that these, without Torah study, will produce, at best, personal emotional health. Understand me: Personal health is necessary, but it is not the end goal for a Jew. We have the additional responsibility of national health.

To ensure our survival, what is in our hands to slow is assimilation, and what is in our hands to grow is Torah study.

Told You So

BECHUKOTAI

I like that little light. You know the one on the dashboard, next to the *E* for empty. It's just a warning. When it lights up, I know I still have a good ten miles' worth of fuel...at least. A few more drives to work, carpool runs, a grocery shop. That light works for me; it's not urgent. It gives me space to consider refueling.

Then there's the flashing light and incessant dinging when your seat belt isn't fastened. It has the urgent feel of a smoke alarm, like there's imminent danger. "I'm just backing out of the driveway!" I tell the car. "I'll put my seatbelt on in a sec." The ding shows no mercy. "Okay. Okay." I resentfully pull the belt across my lap. "Happy now?"

That warning bothers me, because it's like the car is saying, "I don't trust you to use good judgment. I need to see you put that on now." So how about when I toss groceries into the passenger seat? And the dinging starts? Hello...Potatoes don't need a seat belt. Whose judgment should we trust here?

My husband would say the reason I'm bothered by the persistent dinging is because I like to do things when I'm "good and ready." He's right. I don't like to be told I need to do something right now, with no time to think, no time to feel I'm deciding. Of course, that attitude has led me more than once to run out of gas…Well, I wasn't ready to change my plans for the day just to stop at a gas station! Still, there's nobody else to blame for my failure to heed the warning. The warning is clear and the consequences known.

The automobile manufacturer can say, "I told you so."

If anyone has every reason to say, "I told you so," it would be God. In *Parashat Bechukotai*, at the end of *Sefer Vayikra*, we are informed that blessings flow when we follow Hashem's guide to life, and we are clearly warned that bad stuff happens if we don't follow Hashem's guidance.

Every day is about choosing life—or not. We can make the choice to fasten our seatbelts and refuel. The fuel is like Torah study, and we need regular fueling. We need to know when we're running out of steam, and fill 'er up before we become stranded.

The seatbelt is like prohibitions—keeping us safe from dangers of the streets, protected from the destructive consequences of our own mistakes and those of others. For this we need incessant dinging and immediate awareness, until we take action to protect ourselves.

So God has clearly warned us. And we have often clearly failed to heed the warnings—and we face the consequences of our stubbornness.

So why doesn't God say "I told you so?" Hashem is ever-patient with His faith in us. In the event that we do not heed His warnings, He sets us up to take responsibility for our misdeeds.

Time is short. The warning light is on—the one I like. It is a reminder to refuel for my own sake and for the sake of those coming along for the ride. I need to regularly be reinspired in my dedication to Torah living, because I do not want to be up a creek without a paddle, or on the way to school without fuel.

BAMIDBAR

The Center of Law
and Empathy

BAMIDBAR

The venerable sage Rav Yosef Dov Soloveitchik was awake in his living room in the middle of the night. His caretaker got up and asked the *rav* why he was not in bed. Rav Soloveitchik replied that he could not sleep. The previous day, some people had asked him a *sh'eilah* (halachic question), and he had told them to return the next day for the answer.

"I know what the halachah is, and it will be heartbreaking for them. Therefore, I can't sleep."

In *Sefer Bamidbar*, the Jewish People are counted. But the Jewish People were already counted in *Sefer Shemot*. Rav Yaakov Kamenetsky explains: At the time of the Exodus, the people were counted as one nation. Later, in *Bamidbar*, the people were counted each according to his tribe. In the early stages of our nationhood, we needed to be counted as a whole. Then the *Mishkan* was established. The *Mishkan* was the unifying space for building a relationship with Hashem, and once unified, the people could be counted as separate factions that would develop unique strengths as part of Am Yisrael.

In other words:

- First we needed to see ourselves as one big family with a shared focus.
- Then our individual development would be anchored with higher purpose.

If we had been counted as separate tribes before the process of constructing the *Mishkan*, we would be in danger of growing as twelve nationalities struggling against one another to maintain individuality at any cost. Taking Rav Kamenetsky's explanation further, just as smaller factions will break away from the whole if there is not a recognized common goal—with the bottom line that all the tribes will follow God's will—what's to stop each individual from disregarding any whole in favor of the self? Without a common acknowledged center and practical guidelines for maintaining that center, fractionation escalates. The system falls apart, and each individual is left with nothing but his own desires.

We get what we care for.

Our solid center, represented by the *Mishkan*, is service to Hashem, and its practical guidelines are halachah. Rav Soloveitchik could not sleep. Surely, he had turned the halachic question over in his mind. Certainly, he had delved into the text and consulted with other rabbis. Probably, he had struggled to find a way within the *mesorah* to permit what it was these people wanted.

Why didn't he decide to simply disregard the halachah and tell the individuals what they wanted to hear? That would avoid the heartbreak, and he would get some sleep. But Rav Soloveitchik cared too much about the individuals to permit what God does not. He knew that the potential of the individual is inextricably enmeshed with the potential of the whole, both of which are achieved by following halachah. He knew that individuality without halachah leaves one lost, which is worse than any heartbreak.

So why was Rav Soloveitchik disturbed? He should have been able to sleep soundly in the knowledge that he was guiding Jews according to Hashem's law. Here's where we can learn to hold ourselves differently than we hold others. If the ruling had been for himself, the *rav* could choose to be comforted, even joyous, at the prospect of submitting his will to Hashem's. As I once overheard our adolescent child relate to her younger sibling, "Just because you're sad doesn't mean it's bad."

After all, the *rav* was giving the people who had come to him an opportunity to observe the details of their relationship with God above all else. Yet, this thought was not comfort enough to let Rav Soloveitchik sleep.

This is because the ruling was not for himself. While Torah leaders move themselves to accept and appreciate Jewish law as sacred, they also move themselves to share the burdens of individuals experiencing difficult feelings.

The lesson of the *Mishkan* first, before the counting, tells me to keep halachah as the basis of purposeful living. It also means being sensitive to the feelings of others as individuals, because individuals were counted too. And as the *rav* unwittingly displayed, one must not negate the other. In an effort to care for a friend, I must not disregard the ultimate foundation for actualizing potential. And that means, sometimes, not being able to sleep.

> While Torah leaders move themselves to accept and appreciate Jewish law as sacred, they also move themselves to share the burdens of individuals experiencing difficult feelings.

Associate Members

BAMIDBAR

You can learn much about a person by the company he keeps. I advise anyone looking into a prospective spouse to check out the friends. Who are they hanging out with? With what kind of values do their friends live? Do those values reinforce their values? With what kind of community do they associate?

In *Pirkei Avot*, we're enjoined, "*Al tifrosh min ha'tzibbur*—Don't separate from the community." Yet in *Parashat Bamidbar*, Hashem tells Moshe to do something that separates a whole tribe from the rest of the community. A census is taken of the men over twenty years old. "However," Hashem instructs Moshe, "do not count the tribe of Levi."

Rashi offers this: Hashem knew that in the future, the counted ones would die in the desert. However, no one from the tribe of Levi would die because they had not been involved in the sin of the golden calf. It seems *Rashi* is saying that if the tribe of Levi was counted, they'd have to die, because Hashem already decided that the counted ones will not live to enter Israel.

Question: Can't God just decide to count Levi *and* make them live?

Answer: Of course.

Next question: Why didn't He?

Next answer: Maybe Hashem wants us to learn this lesson: Unless one's merits are extremely outstanding, he will suffer the consequences of the community with which he associates.

At first, this seems unfair. Why should I be punished for what those around me are doing?

Simple answer: If I believe I am separate from you, I will never get my head around the idea that the community's lacking brings me suffering. If I know we are all one, I understand why Hashem put a system into place whereby your actions affect my quality of life, and I can grasp the concept of a team win and a team loss. I can understand that even when I play well, my team can lose. I can understand the importance of choosing to join a team with a reputation for winning.

The individuals in the tribe of Levi formed their own "team." They stayed away from the "losing" team that made a golden calf, and thus earned the reward of living through the forty years in the desert and entering into the land of Israel.

This explains their disqualification as part of the general census. It is worth noting that Levi himself, before his descendants became a tribe, was not always praiseworthy. When Levi got together with Shimon, it was they who slew all the men in the city of Shechem after their sister, Dina, was defiled. Their father, Yaakov, was *not* pleased, to say the least. Also, it was Shimon and Levi who decided to kill Yosef, before Reuven convinced them to throw him in a pit instead.

Somewhere along the way, Levi's descendants realized that Shimon was not a good *shidduch* (partner) for them, and when the majority of Jews were heading down the wrong road, the tribe of Levi, as a whole, headed up the right one.

What of *"Al tifrosh min ha'tzibbur"*? Aren't we not supposed to separate from the community? That Mishnah clearly means that we shouldn't separate from a community that is basically winning. The only reason to separate is if the community is clearly heading away from Torah—and even then, don't go solo.

Rabbi Chaim Shmuelevitz notes that just as an entire community can be punished for the demerits of the majority, so the merits of the community carry a favorable judgment for all, including the ones who may not personally merit such favor. In other words, even if I don't always play well, my team can win. And I can be deemed worthy by association.

Of Hair and Wine

NASO

In Parashat Naso, we meet the *nazir*. The *nazir* is a person who, in the times of the Beit Hamikdash, in an effort to elevate his spiritual status, makes a vow to abstain from wine products, haircuts (his own), and burials (of others). When his *nezirut* is over, he brings a *korban chatat*—sin offering. Then he shaves his hair, and it's burned under the pot of the *korban shelamim*—peace offering. (Cool.)

The *nazir* needed to bring a sin offering to atone for the mitzvot he missed by not drinking wine (e.g., Kiddush and Havdalah). Although his intention in becoming a *nazir* was good, he needed to recognize that abstention is not the ideal way of life. The ideal way for a Jew to live is to enjoy the pleasures of this world in their proper context, with the appreciation that they are from God and for God. The reason a person would bring a *korban shelamim* was to show gratitude to God. It is called a peace offering, because expressions of appreciation create peace in the world.

Shelamim also means "wholeness." When a person enjoys God's blessings with gratitude, he is fusing the spiritual with the physical. He is holding two seemingly separate parts together, and that is wholeness. Out of all the sacrifices, the *shelamim* is the one most enjoyed in this world. It has plenty of meat for the one who brought it and the facilitating Kohen to eat and enjoy.

But why burn the hair of the *nazir* under the *shelamim*? For the *nazir*, letting his hair grow and shaving it at the conclusion of his *nazir*-hood were both about not being concerned with beautifying his physical appearance.[1] The *shelamim* was brought as an appreciation for the physical. By abstaining from wine, the *nazir* missed out not only on performing certain mitzvot, but on opportunities to express gratitude for enjoying the physical aspects of those mitzvot.

I wonder if by burning his hair it's a reminder to the *nazir* to start again. You let your hair grow because you needed an extreme reminder to distance from the physicality you got too involved in. Now that you're ready to move back into life as someone involved in the physical world again, it's time to start afresh. This time, you'll know your involvement in physical aspects of life are meant to uplift you to bring you closer to Hashem. You will neither shun them completely nor be involved to the point of forgetting their purpose. Now your hair will begin to grow, and you will regularly care for it so that your appearance can reflect your dignity.

The concept of *nazir*-hood—its restrictions and the rituals for reemergence—can remind us to keep our fingers on the pulse of our material involvements. We want those involvements to be as peace offerings, with plenty to enjoy in service of the One Who provides all things material.

---

1   Rabbi Moshe Weissman, *The Midrash Says: The Book of Bamidbar* (Benei Yaakov Publications, 1983), pp. 75–76.

A Second Chance to Know

BEHAALOTECHA

Dear all,

Regards from sunny Cape Town, South Africa!

Wednesday, I slammed into the recognition of human greatness with overwhelming force.

And too late.

If only I had known before. I thought of Yaakov Avinu after he slept on Har HaMoriah, the site of the future Beit Hamikdash: "Behold, Hashem is in this place, and I did not know."

My husband and I spent the day in Johannesburg. Our first planned meetings were with two powerful personalities: Rabbi Kurtstag, the head of the rabbinical court of South Africa, and Chief Rabbi Warren Goldstein.

In the Chief Rabbi's waiting room, I greeted the secretary, promptly plopped myself on the couch, and closed my jet-lagged eyes, hoping the effects of that just-downed cup of coffee would soon kick in—and not "just now." A moment later, in an attempt to wake myself up, I peeked under heavy eyelids to scan the room for good reading material.

At the edge of the front desk lay an inviting magazine: Jewish Life. I picked it up and flipped through the pages. The administrator behind the desk, an attractive be'sheiteled woman, told me to keep it.

Just then, Rabbi Goldstein emerged. My husband and I stood to follow him into his office, and I carried the magazine with me.

Later that evening, we flew on to Cape Town. As we were settling into our room at the guest house, I unpacked the Jewish Life magazine. Feeling curious, I skimmed through the readers' letters and a few articles. Each was quite well-written and informative.

One particular article held my interest. The first lines read: "Sink or swim. That is what Tracey Ribeiro's life was reduced to, in the small hours of the morning after her husband Jose was in a devastating car accident that left him quadriplegic."

I glanced at the photograph of the smiling b'sheiteled woman sitting beside her smiling b'kippah'ed husband. The woman looked familiar. An awareness crept over me. I slowly turned to my husband.

"Honey? What's the name of the Chief Rabbi's office administrator?" My husband checked his phone.

I knew the answer before he replied. "Tracey."

Completely floored, I read on: "There, in the hospital room, while the love of her life since she was sixteen, and the father of her four children, fought for his life, Tracey could never have known that over the next years her efforts would need to be herculean or that she would rise to the occasion with formidability and flair to give her children a normal life."

The article went on to describe how Tracey struggled to maintain a routine for her children, the youngest only four months old. How she pulled strength from family and community. How she grew in her commitment to Torah and mitzvot.

And counted blessings: "I kept on reminding my husband to look at what we had to be grateful for: He was alive, we had a great marriage, four beautiful, healthy children, an amazing community and support system, and that he hadn't suffered any brain injury. And, of course, very importantly, we had Hashem to lead and guide us through this situation."

I read on with a desperately emotional sense of having missed out. I had missed the merit of knowing of the awesome Godliness of that woman while I was in her presence.

The Ramban tells us that when the Jewish People were presented with "chok u'mishpat" at a place called Marah, they were taught ideas of conduct. Among those ideas, one was how to withstand adversity. As the Jews were soon to receive the Torah, the obvious question is, why did the Jews need a separate presentation of circumstantial rules of conduct? Why not learn all rules of conduct from the Torah text?

Because the most important ideas of how to live cannot be learned from text. The most integral aspects of being are learned from others. As Pirkei Avot states: "Who is wise? One who learns from all people." Wisdom is a depth of understanding that can only be attained through human interaction with a focus on finding Godliness.

In Parashat Behaalotecha, we learn about Pesach Sheini. If someone was tamei on Pesach, he did not get to partake in the mitzvah of korban Pesach. But it wasn't his fault! He had been involved in a Jewish burial, a chessed shel emet—the ultimate kindness.

Hashem offers him a second chance: You couldn't bring the korban then? I'll let you bring it a month later. Sometimes we miss that initial opportunity—not necessarily because we are irresponsible, but because we are involved in other activities. A korban is an opportunity to come close (karov) to God. A person is meant to be moved by the process—to bring himself up.

I missed the initial opportunity to be moved by Tracey Ribeiro. I was handed a second chance in the form of that article. We live in an age of information overload. Intellectual curiosity can be fed by intravenous Internet, constant and continuous. Yet the soul can starve unless I take time to be moved by the fortitude of others.

And so, holding Jewish Life, I let the overpowering wave of realization crash down. I let myself be shaken by the magnitude of kindness and nobility that could exist within one individual. I let myself feel humbled and moved. And I cried.

For behold, Hashem was in that place, and I did not know.

Take the Mussar and Run

SHELACH

Remember the grading system for behavior on your report card?

E—excellent
S—satisfactory
NI—needs improvement

And then there were the categories:

Respectful of peers…
Uses time wisely…

One category should have been: "Learns from surroundings."

If the *meraglim* who spied out the land of Israel were graded on this, they'd get an "NI."

The spies who checked out the land to see if it really was all it was cracked up to be are criticized. The criticism is usually about their lack of faith in the One Who took them out of Egypt—they should have trusted Hashem.

Actually, though, according to *Rashi*, lack of faith was not their biggest failing: The spies who spoke negatively about the land of Israel saw what had happened to Miriam, Moshe's sister, when she spoke negatively about Moshe, yet they "*lo lakchu mussar*—didn't take rebuke."

This is interesting wording. We can have something offered to us, but we won't take it. Why not? Because we don't want it. Most people don't want rebuke (*mussar*). We don't want to be told what we've done wrong and what we might do wrong. In obvious ways, the spies, as the princes of the tribes, were a select few. When it came to seeking *mussar*, though, in this instance they showed themselves to be like most people.

Miriam, Moshe's sister, had just healed from *tzaraat*, a nasty skin disease associated with depressed spiritual levels. Hashem had laid out the *mussar* for the spies in the form of Miriam's punishment for not discussing her concerns about Moshe's behavior with him directly. Instead she had gone to Aharon, their brother. The spies were given the opportunity to put forth the effort to be conscious, to notice the lesson before them and take precautions to avoid their own negative outcome.

They failed. Either they didn't see that the *mussar* was on offer, or they didn't get that the *mussar* could save them. They did not invest in consciousness, the valuing of self, humility, and the desire to be better, which are all prerequisites for taking rebuke.

It's one thing to be able to accept rebuke, it's another to actively seek it. Seeking rebuke may sound like you're being a glutton for punishment, but in reality, it is quite a pleasant way to live. It's about investing in each moment now so as not to have to deal with mistakes later. Inevitably, mistakes will happen, but if we could have avoided them, we are accountable.

A dear friend of mine is fond of saying, "*Derech aruchah hi ketzarah*—The long way is short." *Mussar* lies all around, and when we invest in enough awareness and energy to take it, our spiritual report card will be something to be proud of!

Red Rover and the Promised Land

SHELACH

When I was a kid, we played a schoolyard game called Red Rover. There were two teams. Team members stood side by side, holding hands. Teams stood thirty or so feet apart, facing each other. One team decided which particular player they wanted to "call over" from the opposing team and then chanted: "Red Rover, Red Rover, we call [particular player] right over."

Then "particular player" would run full force toward the opposing team into one pair of clasped hands, trying to break through the chain. If "pp" successfully broke through, she chose someone from that team to return with her to the team from which she ran. The teams took turns calling people over. The winning team was the team that had the most players when the sudden (upsetting) end-of-recess bell would sound.

The way to maintain a winning team in Red Rover was to hold tightly so as not to let the ones you call over break through. And it was to your benefit to call over strong players who wanted to be on your team. That way they would not fight too hard to break through, and they would hold strong against the next player who tried to break through.

From the time we left Egypt, Hashem was "calling us over." He was inviting us to join His team.

Receiving the Torah at Har Sinai was a huge team-building experience. We all stood together on God's side. Entering the land of Israel was to be the ultimate "calling us over." It was our chance to show that we were ready to live in the practical world with an awareness of being with God. Ideally, when Hashem invited us into His land, we should have surrendered ourselves completely to His will. Faced with the opportunity to enter the Promised Land, we should have simply walked ourselves over to Hashem's side without even trying to break through.

Yet, alas, we are human. This means we are sometimes blind. In our blindness, we can charge toward our security fence with a desire to be free of the constraints that protect us and allow us to grow healthily. And, usually, Hashem will not let us break through. He'll let us push and shove our small selves against Him. And He'll let us exhaust ourselves in our tantrums. And He'll remain unchanging, as we either flail against Him or decide to willingly hold His hand.

> In our blindness, we can charge toward our security fence with a desire to be free of the constraints that protect us and allow us to grow healthily.

In our house, we have a little book entitled *Reasons My Kid Is Crying.* On the front cover is a photograph of a wailing child in the background. In the foreground, a father's fingers hold two pieces of cheese. In parentheses the dad has written reason number 46 that his kid is crying: "I broke this cheese in half."

A few of the other goodies in the book are: "His aunt wouldn't let him play with the axe," "His swimsuit got wet." And, my personal favorite, "I wouldn't let him play with the dead squirrel he found in the yard."

For parents and grandparents of toddlers this book is therapy. While it is completely expected and even appropriate for a two-year-old to freak out at the drop of a hat (or the split of the cheese), not so for older children and adults. Children need behavioral guidance when it comes to expressing frustration. They will not initially understand that our decisions are best for them.

And we need not expect their understanding; only their appropriate behavior. In time, however, if people are to be healthy, they must grow trust. They must trust enough not to fret over circumstances out of their control and opportunities offered by those with a good track record.

The Jews were just outside the land of Israel. They had left Egypt amid signs and wonders, crossed the sea in a miraculous sweep of God's protection, and experienced the most powerful revelation of God's commitment. The next step was the opportunity to settle the Promised Land. And what did the Jews do? They threw a tantrum!

Ten of the twelve spies entered the land unfaithfully. And upon their return, and their evil report, the congregation (except the women and the Levi'im) wailed in utter fear and hopelessness. They were as toddlers, with no understanding of what was good for them. And so they cried.

Although when Hashem "called us over" to His land, he wanted us to join His team...now, He "loosened His grip." He let individuals break through and take others back to the other side. He was teaching us that if we completely leave trust out of the picture, if we tantrum with complete lack of faith and an absolute resolution to not stand with Him, He will allow us to experience the consequences—and He will suspend the original offer.

Daily challenges are Hashem's way of calling us over. Let's hope that through our responses to challenge, Hashem will detect our desire to be on His team. Let's hope He holds His "hands" securely in place so that, at worst, we will only exhaust ourselves in the attempt to break through or wriggle our way out. And, at best, we will charge full force toward Him, with every intention of surrendering ourselves, before the end-of-recess-bell sounds.

In Pursuit

KORACH

What evades us when we actively seek it, yet finds us when we purposely avoid it?

We live in a society that tempts us to "tweet" and "status update" our every activity. We can be lured into thinking that our actions only have value when they are recognized by others, but this way of thinking can pull us far from our best selves.

Forty years before the Jewish People first entered the land of Israel as a nation, a man named Korach did not recognize his own worth. He sought recognition. He rallied men behind him. He convinced them that they too deserved more recognition, which in actuality pulled them away from the true source of worthiness. A rebellion ensued. The end came swiftly, and it was not pretty.

The seed of the pursuit of honor is the misperception that we do not have innate worth. This leads us to destructively thinking that our deeds are inconsequential. Then we either fall into depression or desperately hunt down fleeting sources of proof of our worth (i.e., posting every moment's movements or kick-starting rebellions). There is a better way to be.

"Honor" is the answer to the opening question. The most honorable people are those who accomplish without seeking recognition.[1] They live with the understanding that they matter. Their actions matter. They do not need to seek credit for their every effort. My wise father is fond of quoting "If you don't care who gets the credit, you can accomplish so much!" Easier said than done; we like when our accomplishments are recognized.

What to do?

How do we balance our desire for recognition with our genuine quest to better ourselves?

A few ideas that might have helped Korach and can help us now:

- Give honor where honor is due: Honor, like love, cannot be taken—only given and received. Since we cannot control what will be ours to receive, the way to be connected to honor is to give it.
- Accept honor with an understanding that you are giving others the opportunity to give, and let yourself feel thankful that you were able to put forth the effort necessary to accomplish.
- Every day, do a kindness that nobody knows about. And don't mess it up by trying to pretend it doesn't matter. Let go of the voice that says, "Well, that's just the garbage. Anybody can take that out." That is the voice of Korach, the voice that undermines your worth.

When we accept our humanness and continuously push ourselves just beyond it, we will experience a gradual shift in our desire for recognition, as it begins to melt into our quest to actually be a better person.

That undermining voice will not help you to keep up your daily run, your healthy routine. Instead, tell

---

1   *Pirkei Avot* 4:1.

yourself that your actions matter. Let yourself feel proud that you can take action without needing recognition from others! This will exercise that selfless/worthy muscle. When we accept our humanness and continuously push ourselves just beyond it, we will experience a gradual shift in our desire for recognition, as it begins to melt into our quest to actually be a better person.

Then our status will change naturally over time, without any posted updates.

Clever Women,
Wise Wives

KORACH

It is 1312 BCE. The *parashah* opens with four instigators: Korach, brothers Datan and Aviram, and Ohn ben Pelet.

Ohn is never again mentioned in the text. What happened to him? The Gemara in Sanhedrin tells a fascinating tale:[1]

- Ohn is convinced to join Korach, to rebel against Moshe and Aharon. He is swayed by the argument that all men are holy; anyone can be the leader.

- Ohn's wife knows that Korach's rebellion is wrong. She also knows Ohn is attracted to the prospect of moving up the "corporate" ladder. Ohn's wife beseeches her husband to bow out of the mutinous activities.

---

1   109b.

- Ohn doesn't. Appealing to her husband's thirst for power, Mrs. Ben Pelet reminds her husband that if the rebellion succeeds, Korach will be a leader, while Ohn will still be a follower. Ohn realizes the wisdom of his wife, but behaves cowardly and takes no action to secede from the planned rebellion.
- Mrs. B. swings into action. She serves her husband alcohol until he falls asleep. Then she situates herself outside the entrance of their tent. Korach and the 250 rebels are headed in the direction of Ohn's tent. The Mrs. unwraps her long hair and proceeds to brush it attractively.
- Korach notices Mrs. Ben Pelet with her uncovered hair. Korach and the mob quickly turn away to avoid Ohn's tent. Ohn is not pulled into the confrontation.
- The Mrs. retreats. Mission accomplished. So far.

This story never fails to intrigue me. Marriage is about creating a space in which your spouse can grow into his best self. When we make marriage our most important human relationship, our decisions are about creating that space. Were Ohn to have joined the rebellion, he would not have been able to grow into his best self. Something had to be done. The Mrs. had already urged her husband to walk away from the rebellion, but Ohn took no action.

Mrs B. could have done what women have done for centuries, much to the chagrin of their husbands: She could have nagged him. "Ohn, what's your problem? Hashem chose Moshe and Aharon to lead us. Go tell Korach you want out. Go ahead, tell him now. Why are you just sitting here? Get up. Go." And on and on, she could have nagged.

Nagging does not create a peaceful home. And wise people do not repeat behaviors that have failed to achieve results. They try different approaches until they find one that works. Seeing that her husband was not going to extricate himself, Mrs. Ben Pelet shifted her focus. She considered the priorities of the opponent. She thought, *Korach envisions himself as holy enough to be the Kohen Gadol. Surely, he knows that a man who would expose himself to a public display of immodesty would never be accepted as Kohen Gadol.* Mrs. B. knew what she was up against.

Her weapon of choice involved a temporary loss of pride, but she risked that loss for the greater gain.

And, soon enough, the earth swallowed the rebels, whose deaths became a lesson to be learned from, for all time.

A woman needs to be wise to feed her marriage.

Around the year 90 CE, a woman named Rachel wanted her husband, Akiva, to learn Torah. Akiva would need to sit in a room full of young children to learn the *aleph-bet*. At forty years old, her husband was embarrassed. Rachel could have nagged him. "I gave up a fortune to marry you. My father disowned me. You'd better get out and start learning!" Rachel did not nag, but still, something had to be done. She considered the priorities of the opponent. In this case, the opponent was Akiva's own *yetzer hara*, which was promoting destructive embarrassment.

To create an opening for the space in which her husband would grow closer to his best self, Rachel had a plan. She gathered handfuls of soil and placed them onto a donkey's back. She planted flowers in that soil. She asked her devoted husband to please do her a favor and walk the streets with this donkey.

At first, bystanders scoffed at the sight of Akiva and the flowerbed donkey. Until people simply got used to the sight. Soon, their mocking ceased. Akiva realized that the same would happen if he studied with five-year-olds. And the rest is history.

Rachel knew what she was up against. Her weapon of choice involved a temporary loss of pride. Yet, soon enough, Akiva became an undisputed sage whose life became a lesson to be learned from, for all time.

When we know the purpose of marriage, we can commit to fulfilling it. We can gather our courage and exert the necessary energy toward becoming people who carry the inspiration of those who have lived before.

We can pull ourselves out from that unproductive, temporarily comfortable place, into the space that provides lessons to be learned. And if we live wisely enough, our considerations and actions will become attached to the eternal. For all time.

Greetings

CHUKAT

Miriam the prophetess, and her brother Aharon, the Kohen Gadol, pass away, and the loss is tremendous. The people will need to let go. Goodbyes are associated with letting go.

Yet it's not only goodbyes that are about letting go. Greetings, too, include letting go. To greet another wholeheartedly involves letting go of my stuff. It's about making the interaction focused on the other. I need to let go of the desire to be attended to, and hold on to the idea of attending to another.

Thomas Edison decided on the "Hello" to say when we answer the phone. Apparently, Alexander Graham Bell wanted us to say, "Ahoy hoy." (Some people should stick to inventing revolutionary technological devices.) Today, a person checks the caller ID to see who's calling and picks up with a "Hey." E-mails and texts begin with the fifth letter of the Hebrew alphabet too.

We used to be interested in finding out who was calling us. The "Hello" was with respectful curiosity. I am not going to wax nostalgic for bygone days of greater respect. I believe that Hashem gives us the ingredients we need to embrace each other respectfully in every generation.

So what keeps us from greeting another wholeheartedly? Perhaps we sometimes fear that if we greet others with gusto, they might think that our lives are perfect, which would deprive us of sympathy, comfort, recognition of our struggles, and other variations on that theme.

> Perhaps we sometimes fear that if we greet others with gusto, they might think that our lives are perfect, which would deprive us of sympathy, comfort, recognition of our struggles, and other variations on that theme.

I am not suggesting that we deny our need for these real validations. Only that we not seek them constantly. That we see ourselves as givers. While many may naturally think that gift-getting is the best blessing, a Torah lifestyle reminds us otherwise.

At Tali Ross's bat mitzvah in South Africa, I merited to receive a blessing from Miri Ehrental, the woman who founded the organization Zichron Menachem. After losing their fourteen-year-old son to cancer, she and her husband rose from their pain to establish an address in Israel for families living with cancer.

Miri looked me squarely in the eyes. "May you be *zocheh* (merit) to be a giver and not a taker!"

We have a great opportunity to consider our friends before we answer a phone call. We have a chance to brighten a moment in the way we greet another person. And the great thing about caller ID? The caller can know that you answered cheerfully knowing it was him or her. It's like saying "Ahoy hoy" to you for being you!

Be Little and Sing

BALAK

The sweet kindergarten voices are singing, "*Mah tovu ohalecha Yaakov*—How good are your tents, Jacob, *mishkenotecha Yisrael*—your dwellings, Israel." In their innocence, the children are clueless regarding the origin of these words, which remind us that nothing happens without Hashem.

King Balak of Moav fears that the Jewish People who are encamped in the desert near his land will rise up to attack his country. He plots to get Bilaam, a gentile prophet, to curse the Jews in order to weaken them enough so that King Balak and his army can defeat them. The Torah uses three different Hebrew root words for the word "curse" in Balak's exchanges with Bilaam. One root word was particularly unfamiliar to me. I could not recall ever coming across it. The root is *kuf-bet* (*kav*).

Rabbi Hirsch often comments on the etymology of words in the Torah. He says that because the word *nakav* means to "make a hole," the word *kavav* would mean to "hollow out." Along those lines, Rabbi Hirsch also points out that the word *kav* (with a letter *bet*) is a measure of capacity commonly used in the Talmud.

One other place in *Chumash* that the root *kav* is used is in *Parashat Emor*, regarding the person who blasphemed God. What does it mean to blaspheme? Blasphemy is the attempt to profane that which is sacred—to make hollow that which is filled.

So this word for "curse" is particularly related to speaking to or about someone in a manner that "hollows" them out. If you have ever been the target of a person with the intent to belittle you, you know that feeling "hollow" rings painfully true as a description of what that person's words have done to you.

Here's the thing: That person's intent is just that—just intent. It does not have to play out as reality. And the episode here with Bilaam reinforces that truth. You see, Bilaam was intending to curse/hollow out the Jewish People with his words. Try as he might, only words of praise and blessing fell from his lips. During his first attempt to curse the Jews, Bilaam uttered the following: "How can I curse/hollow out what has not been hollowed out by God? How can I doom what is not doomed by God?"[1] And during Bilaam's final attempt to curse the Jews, he said, "*Mah tovu ohalecha Yaakov…*"[2]

I'd like to suggest that whenever we come across a person with a pattern of belittling others, we remember the words, "How can you hollow out one who is not hollowed out by God?"

In other words, I am filled with meaning. I have God in me. Your words cannot hollow me.

> I am filled with meaning. I have God in me. Your words cannot hollow me.

And what irony! The words from a man intending to belittle and undermine the potential of our nation's growth toward goodness turn out to be a staple of our morning prayers. Those words are belted out by the youngest members of our congregation—the ones happy to be little in the way that they are filled with massive potential for blessed growth.

---

1   *Bamidbar* 23:8.
2   Ibid., 24:5.

Faith with Desire

PINCHAS

The daughters of a man named Tzelafchad so desired the Land that they approached Moshe directly with their request: Our father has died. There are no sons. Please, when we enter the Land of Israel and land is divvied up, can we inherit our father's land?

While this is the only time we meet these women in the text, they are mentioned by a sixteenth-century commentator—the *Kli Yakar*, Rabbi Shlomo Efraim Luntschitz—four *parshiyot* earlier, in *Parashat Shelach*: Hashem tells Moshe, "*Shelach lecha anashim*—Send for yourself men" to spy the Land.[1] One of the explanations the *Kli Yakar* gives here is that Hashem was telling Moshe that Moshe could send men, if he so desired, but that Hashem's choice would be to send women. The commentator goes on to say that in particular, God would choose Tzelafchad's daughters to spy out the Land, because in the future they would display their desire for the Land.

---

1   *Bamidbar* 13:2.

(Before we women get all haughty, it might be useful to note that immediately preceding this reason for the wording "*Shelach lecha anashim*," the *Kli Yakar* writes, "Send men who will not be like women who gossip." Yeah, so there's that.)

Some ideas about desire:

- For desire to take root, there needs to be distance between the person and the object of desire. (I do not yearn for that which I have just acquired.)
- There also needs to be discomfort regarding the distance. I may be far from Antarctica, but if I am not bothered by that fact, I will not desire to be there.
- If I am desiring something that is realistically attainable, and I believe I am worthy of the benefits of that attainment, my desire can fuel my efforts in that direction.

In the case of *bnot Tzelafchad* desiring the Land of Israel—and all the women in *Parashat Shelach*, for that matter, who were not swayed by the biased reporting of ten fearful spies—what might we say the women were desiring that the men were not? Although *emunah* (faith) is a term often relied upon to describe the women who trusted that Hashem would deliver the Land of Canaan into their hands, it is not the description given here by the *Kli Yakar* to explain why Hashem would have chosen women to spy out the Land. The reason given is not faith; it is desire.

Desire for what? What is it about the Land that the women desired?

If we picture the women as faithful to Hashem, we might be tempted to say that they desired the closeness to God that they could feel in the Promised Land. We, with our ever-retro(spective) insight, know that Eretz Yisrael is the place to most intensely experience Hashem's presence.

Still, it is difficult to defend the idea that the women wanted to settle the Land to feel closer to God. After all, daily life in the *midbar* (desert) during the Jews' sojourns was the most apparent smorgasbord of God's mastery over nature and involvement in life. There were the cushioning clouds below the people's feet, preventing injury from harsh desert sand, snakes, scorpions, and the like; plus the clouds surrounding the camp, which provided insulation from harsh weather conditions and wild animals. There were perfect streams of water for drinking, clothing that miraculously never needed washing, perfect nourishment in the form of *mann* that fell from the sky, for God's sake! Can you imagine a material existence any more assuring of Hashem's involvement in our lives, let alone His existence?

So we return to the question: What was it the women were desiring about the Land? And how might it have been related to *emunah*? We know that closeness to God is the source of all yearning, so let's circle back to the idea of desiring closeness. We have just established that there was quite apparent closeness to God in the desert experience. The fact that the women desired a different experience can mean that they desired a different closeness. Instead of a closeness that was simply a given, perhaps they yearned for a closeness they partnered to create.

A comparison might be useful here. A nursing mother and baby are close—intensely so. There is no doubt that Baby is fully dependent on Mama; the closeness is undeniably and absolutely apparent. This closeness feels good to Baby. Baby has no desire, initially, to experience any other closeness. That closeness is just fine, thanks. Soon enough, though, Baby begins to experience stirrings of independence—the willingness to jeopardize the given closeness, at least temporarily, for the idea of something else. If we can identify that something else, we will begin to understand the nature of the women's desire to live in the land.

It cannot be that the women simply wanted to be independent of apparent care. A very young child only wants his needs met. As a child grows, though, he wants more than to know he is cared for. A healthy child wants to know he can care for himself too, and later, to care for others. He wants to be capable. In order to become capable of caring for himself and others, he must try to do just that. He must risk leaving his mother's care in that process. If mother and child are basically healthy, mother will allow and even delight in the child's venture. The mother will compliment the child for the effort, so the child can develop a bedrock of trust in himself that he will need in order to continue venturing thoughtfully into the adventure of living apart from mom, tending to himself and others.

Going back to the idea of yearning for a different closeness, what kind of closeness is the one achieved through this process? I want to suggest that this closeness is a closeness of trust. It is a basic desire to be cared for and tended to. It is a different desire to be trusted. For the first desire to be fulfilled, I depend on another. It requires no exertion on my part to become anything other than who I already am. For the second desire to be fulfilled, I need to become something. I need to become trustworthy. In order to become worthy of trust, I need to venture out and little by little establish patterns of reliability and accountability in different aspects of life.

The opportunity to become trustworthy begins with my desire to be trusted. That desire can unfortunately fuel me to try to fool, guilt, or manipulate you into thinking that there is something wrong with you if you don't trust me. Alternatively, on a healthier route, that desire will fuel me to become a person of integrity—a person who values honest engagement with himself and the world, a person who takes responsibility for continuously aligning himself with Godly values.

I want to suggest that it was this—becoming trustworthy—that the women were desiring. While the men were good with being cared for—perhaps worrying about the inevitable failure that they would experience in becoming trustworthy—the women desired a new connection. The women wanted a connection born of uncertainty, because the outcome depended on their own efforts.

Living in the Land meant leaving the connection of the certainty of God's tending, and here's where faith comes in. In order to leave certainty and succeed in the uncertain terrain of human effort, we need faith, *emunah*. We need to have faith that we have what it takes—not necessarily to succeed, but to keep getting up after every fall, through harsh conditions, painful stings, messy garments, and lack of nourishment. When we desire closeness, and we cannot control what others may or may not do to/for us, where will we turn? What will we have to rely upon? Faith—in our capacity to care for ourselves and others in a Godly way.

And then the relationship with Hashem changes—just as a child grows an appreciation for his parents when he leaves home, and even more so when he becomes a parent himself. That is when he realizes the depth of complex considerations that go into tending for a life. And in becoming trustworthy, the child learns what it means to be faithful. Not only in the sense of being loyal, but in believing that others can also develop faith in themselves and others. And the cycle continues.

Simply stating that the women possessed more *emunah* than the men, and therefore didn't believe the spies and wanted to enter the land, could minimize the depth of the women's desire: to connect to Hashem by being more like Him, being faithful through the times and spaces of seeming distance.

To grow up is to strive to be Godly. To only desire to be tended to is to never grow up. And though it does seem that plan A in Gan Eden was for God to care in a very obvious manner for His creations, the first woman's desire for a different connection to God brought us to where we are now. Chavah desired to be more like Hashem, to experience broader independence and decision-making capacity. Although we can say that it was this desire that led to the downfall of mankind, it seems it's this desire that could rectify that downfall.

And in the world of plan B, Machlah, Noa, Chaglah, Milkah, and Tirtzah, the daughters of Tzelafchad, each got a shout-out in the text. They also have their genealogy traced back to Yosef, who not only loved the Land of Israel, but clearly lived with *emunah* and desire to act with faithfulness through times of seeming distance.

Just as our souls were fully tended to by Hashem before we were conceived into this world, so will we be fully enveloped in His tenderness after our souls leave this world. In the meantime, we receive small sparks of that tenderness in the periodic spaces of feeling full acceptance by our soulful selves and our loved ones. Yet the vast majority of space in our lives is made meaningful by our efforts toward becoming trustworthy.

When we notice that those efforts stem from a deep desire to have *emunah*, we can give ourselves shout-outs in the texts of our minds and credit our faithfulness to those who preceded us.

Filtered Projections

MATOT

There are two Hebrew words that both mean "tribe." Those same words also both mean "branch" or "stick." The words are *shevet* (pl. *shevatim*) and *mateh* (pl. *matot*).

Parashat Matot, in the context of the first verse, refers to the tribes of Israel.

"Moshe spoke to the heads of the tribes of the children of Israel saying, 'This is what Hashem has commanded.'"[1] The Lubavitcher Rebbe, Rabbi Menachem Mendel Schneerson, explained that thin, pliable branches are called *shevatim* when they are still attached to the tree, and those same branches are called *matot* when they are detached. The fact that the tribes are being addressed as *matot* here reminds us that Hashem allows us—in a sense—to detach from Him. And then He offers us His guidance, and we strike out on our own. And we mess up—a lot.

I wonder at Hashem allowing people to make such a mess of this world. Then, in the same wondering, I am awestruck by Hashem's continuous

---

1   *Bamidbar* 30:2.

186 Up to God

faith in us. He keeps granting us access to His Torah, the instruction manual for every circumstance and aspect of ourselves. God's Torah is eternal and complete. Human beings are limited and incomplete, yet Torah can only live in this world through human beings. So when Torah lives through us, we could say that Torah appears limited and incomplete. How does Hashem stand for His beloved, perfect Torah to appear somewhat skewed as it is filtered through us mortals?

It's like a master painter, who leaves detailed instructions for replication of his masterpiece and entrusts those instructions to a class of preschool children. He knows that none of those children's paintings will truly reflect his original, so why not just hang the original masterpiece to be admired for posterity? That way, all will know of the greatness of that painter!

Hashem has a different plan. He does not want us to know only of His greatness, He also wants to give us the opportunity to create our own greatness, and in doing so, to become more like Him, and therefore closer to Him. Because Torah is eternal and complete, when we live with Torah, we become less limited and more complete. So Hashem risks having His Torah appear flawed so that we can become greater! How crazy is that! It's like He puts His reputation on the line so that we can grow!

What can I take from this epiphany? Think about this: Why am I hesitant to allow a child to set the table when guests are due to arrive? Because I know that the child will not set the table exactly as I would, and I worry that the setting will reflect badly on me. Where are my priorities? If I hope to draw that child toward less limitations and more wholeness and closer to me, I will encourage the child to "help" even when it does not seem so helpful. God Himself allows His most precious possession (Torah!) to be carried by our deeply flawed, inept selves! Am I more perfect than God Himself in demanding that anything that reflects me must be completely me?! If so, I remain far from Godliness, limited by the image I wish to project.

I will never forget the story told by a dear friend of ours about a rebbetzin who opened her front door one evening to find a well-respected donor of her husband's yeshiva standing there. Her small Israeli apartment was buzzing with the routine activities of many children. The woman greeted her unexpected, distinguished guest and began introducing him to each of the children in order of appearance. Just then, the bathroom door swung open, and one sixteen-year-old boy, a severely socially challenged child, stumbled out into the hallway in a half-soaked bathrobe, wearing steamed-up, lopsided eyeglasses and an inside-out yarmulke perched crookedly on his dripping, still soapy hair. What happened next is what inspires me to retell this story. Without a moment's hesitation, without a hint of apology, the rebbetzin put her arm around her son's shoulders and smiled with genuine pride. Then she introduced her son as if he had just won the Nobel Prize: "This is my son Moshe!"

When we can overlook what we deem as ineptitude on the part of others and allow them to contribute to the picture of our lives, we give reason for Hashem to continue having faith in us.

The Safety of Kindness

MAS'EI

"And the cities that you provide for yourselves shall be six cities of refuge. Three cities you will provide on the other side of the Jordan, and three cities you will provide in the Land..."[1]

A city of refuge was a safe place for a man to live if he accidentally killed someone. In the city of refuge, he would be safe from revenge that the dead man's family may want to seek. Two and a half tribes settled on the east side of the Jordan River, just outside Israel. Nine and a half tribes settled inside the borders of the Land of Israel. The Torah instructs the Jews to build three refuge cities inside Israel and three on the east of the Jordan.

Does it make sense to have the same number of cities of refuge for two and a half tribes as for nine and a half tribes? The Talmud offers the explanation that murder was more prevalent on the east bank of the Jordan.

This raises a question that needs some introduction.

---

1   *Bamidbar* 35:13–14.

Rabbi Dov Furer cites an important understanding. When we say that certain neighborhoods have a high murder rate, that's because more people commit murder there. Murder, by definition, is willful. Cities of refuge won't help those people because they are intentional murderers! So what is the Talmud telling us by saying that east of the Jordan needed more cities of refuge per capita? Can accidental killings be prevalent?

That is the question. And the answer lies in the fact that Hashem instructs us to build the same number of refuge cities for two and a half tribes as for nine and a half tribes. Yes—accidental killings can be prevalent. In a place where murder is prevalent, the value of human life is diminished. In such an atmosphere, people may be less inclined to take precautions to preserve life. With less precautions to preserve life, more accidents will happen.

Taking precautions is an aspect of basic kindness.

When the Jewish women were giving birth in Egypt, in the latest stages of slavery, bringing children into what seemed to be a hopelessly doomed environment, there labored Jewish midwives.

How many midwives does it take to deliver a Jewish baby in Mitzrayim? Two. Shifra and Puah (otherwise known as Yocheved and Miriam or Yocheved and Elisheva):

Shifra and Puah (otherwise…Elisheva): one to do the delivering and the other to swaddle and coo.

The first provides conditions for living, while the second provides kindness.

The details of the midwives' involvement in our darkest hours, just prior to salvation, are not random. The actions of the midwives remind us of what needs to be done if we wish to move beyond darkness. We must ensure the delivery of life, yes. And we must also take precautions against diminished value of life by actively caring for others.

> The actions of the midwives remind us of what needs to be done if we wish to move beyond darkness.

Surely the babies just needed to be delivered? Who needs cooing and swaddling when the future looks so bleak?

We do! We need to say kind words to each other and care for each other to bring meaning to our preservation. In performing caring actions, we move away from the probability of frequent loss of life. Then we'll rarely need to run from danger in search of refuge. For our refuge will be found right in our own homes and communities.

In the form of kindness.

DEVARIM

How It Can Be

DEVARIM

"Eichah—How [can it be that] I alone carry your difficulty and your burdens and your disputes" (*Devarim* 1:12).

"*Eichah*—How [can it be that] she has become a harlot" (*Yeshayahu* 1:21).

"*Eichah*—How [can it be that] she sits alone" (*Megillat Eichah* 1:1).

The word *eichah* denotes a question that escalates into disbelief. *Eichah* is like "What?!" and "How?!" that run through our minds when we face an overwhelmingly painful situation. It is a cry of despair in the form of a question that expresses our struggle to accept that we have lost one reality and now live in another:

- When Moshe Rabbeinu said "*Eichah*" in *Devarim*, which we read this Shabbat, he was addressing the Jewish People before he died. He was reminding them of why he had appointed judges to assist him.

- When Yeshayahu said "*Eichah*" in the haftarah that we read this Shabbat, the prophet was bemoaning the state of the Jewish

People, during the latter times of the First Beit Hamikdash, in the hopes that the Jews would return to Hashem.

- In the third "*Eichah*," the prophet Yirmiyahu was mourning over the desolation of Jerusalem after the destruction of the First Beit Hamikdash.

- On Tishah B'Av we read Yirmiyahu's *Eichah*. The Beit Hamikdash is gone. The loss is massive. On this day, we open the storehouse of all our losses. We unlock the floodgates of all sadness, disappointment, and heartbreak.

The ninth of Av is the day for collective mourning.

We can easily see how Yeshayahu's *Eichah* is connected to Yirmiyahu's *Eichah*. The former recognizes the reason for the latter. Yet Moshe's "*Eichah*," verbalized hundreds of years before, under totally different circumstances, seems unrelated. How is Moshe's questioning statement connected to the other two?

The fact that Moshe uses the word that reminds us of sadness and loss is not coincidence. What was Moshe sad about? And what was lost? *Rashi* tells us that in the desert, with Moshe as the sole judge, the people were unbearably contentious. When one would see that Moshe might judge in favor of his opponent, he'd say, "I have more witnesses to bring." The people would endlessly challenge Moshe's rulings. With this in mind, we can understand why Moshe exclaimed, "*Eichah!*" How can I carry all this stuff?!

It wasn't simply the burden of judging so many people; it was the aggressive way in which the Jews treated one another, even in front of Moshe Rabbeinu!

Sad.

This behavior led Moshe to install other judges. And now the loss—the loss was massive. Moshe Rabbeinu was the closest to Hashem any human being ever was and ever would be! Now the people fell away from contact with the awesomeness of Moshe himself.

This was not the first sad loss where we find "*Eichah*," though. Man's first exile was from Gan Eden. After Adam and Chavah ate from the

Tree of Knowledge of good and evil, they "hid" from Hashem. Hashem called to Adam, "Where are you?"[1]

Think about it:

- God does not need man to tell Him his whereabouts.
- God wants man to hear the question: "Where are you?"

In the scheme of life and your potential, how are you faring? And the word Hashem used is one that should stir us. It is a questioning word with undertones of disappointment and a sublime eternal message of loss. The first experience of loss, which held the seeds of all future loss was this: the loss of closeness to Hashem.

It should not surprise us to find that the Hebrew letters of the word "*Ayekah*—Where are you?" that Hashem asked Adam, are *aleph, yud, kaf, hei*...the same as the word "*Eichah.*" Adam and Chavah disobeyed Hashem's command, they were exiled from Gan Eden, and loss was introduced to the world. And lest we think that wrongdoings of previous generations are irrelevant, we have only to look in the reading of *Devarim*. Here we find Moshe rebuking the people for complaining about not having food, for their fear of leaving Mitzrayim, for building the golden calf, for the sin of the spies, and more.

The problem here is that the men who were actually involved in those particular episodes had already died. The ones Moshe was addressing were the children and grandchildren of those men—the next generation. They were the ones about to enter the Land of Israel to conquer and settle it. And the midrash tells us that not only were the people silent throughout the rebuke, they actually felt regret and accepted responsibility.

About what was their regret? They felt regret for the fact that connection to Hashem was lost, and they took responsibility to repair that loss. They were the generation that merited to conquer and settle the Land.

Wrongdoings of previous generations are relevant for as long as there is loss and lacking. Loss and lack invite us to regret and take responsibility. Tishah B'Av is not yet a festival because we have yet to collectively

---

1   *Bereishit* 3:9.

carry an attitude of intense regret for what has been lost, and to cry out because of it. And we have yet to collectively accept responsibility for the lack of the Beit Hamikdash.

Until such time that we will suffer loss no more, the disbelieving cry of *"Eichah!"* I will direct to the world. And the cry of *"Ayekah—*Where are you?!" I will direct to the one who is accountable for my response. *"Ayekah?"* I will ask myself.

Where Is God's Compassion?

VA'ETCHANAN

The Jews are camped on the east side of the Jordan river. They are preparing to cross the river into Israel. They've been traveling in the desert for forty years with Moshe as their tireless leader. Moshe will not be the one to lead the people into the next integral phase of their peoplehood—the fighting for and settling into the Promised Land. Moshe pleads for God to "change His mind" and let Moshe enter the Land. Hashem tells Moshe, "Stop pleading. Go up to the peak of the mountain, where you will see the whole of the Land that you will not enter. Then, charge Yehoshua and strengthen him and encourage him, because he will pass before these people, and he will make them inherit the Land that you will see."

How hard this must be for Moshe. I wonder, when I read these verses, where is Hashem's compassion? Moshe deeply desires to enter the Holy Land. He is pleading for God's sake! We can imagine the depth of—what

197

is it? Is it hope? Is it despair? Moshe is begging with all his vulnerable, true, longing self. I can picture Moshe on his knees, tears in his eyes, head raised heavenward, hands clenched over his heart. "Please, please, please...Hashem!"

Moshe's mind could be holding valid reasons why he should be granted permission to at least enter the Land:

- All the life-altering experiences I have shared with this people
- All desirable living I have given up for this people—a private life of shepherding a beloved flock, an intimate relationship with my beloved wife
- All the anguish I have suffered worrying about this nation
- All the time defending Hashem's honor to these people
- All the courage I have mustered to protect them
- All the energy I have expended in teaching them and living steadfastly by those teachings

And for what is Moshe asking? Simply for the chance to enter the Land with his people. Maybe help them acclimate to the new reality of apparent separateness from God's provision and protection? We mortals can feel for Moshe.

Here is God, not only refusing Moshe's request, but expecting Moshe to give Yehoshua a leadership workshop, including a reality check about the difficulties of leadership and a pep talk including encouragement to stay with the program. And all the while, Moshe is experiencing the pain of his own exclusion. This expectation seems too much. It's like God is saying, "Get over your pain. Your job now is to prepare Yehoshua to do what you wish you could be doing."

And Moshe would have every right to think, "Hashem, can't a guy catch a break? Can't I just feel sorry for myself for a few minutes? Won't You feel sorry with me? Can't You see I'm heartbroken! I mean, I knew I might not be going into the Land with them, but I didn't know how painful it would feel to be left out at this point. How am I supposed to strengthen Yehoshua when I can barely strengthen myself to accept this blow? And why should it be my job to strengthen Yehoshua?! Why can't You do that the way You did for me? Just tell him Yourself that You'll be with him, like You were with me."

Yet we see no indication of Hashem recognizing anything like that. We can learn something practical and profound from God's (seeming) callousness and Moshe's acceptance here. Any individual who has ever parented or educated knows this: There comes a point at which you stay back, a line you do not cross, a time at which you must accept that you will not be traveling further with the child.

From that line, you do what is best for the child. You give a last-minute reminder of reality with encouraging words, a hug, a smile, a wave. And because of everything that you have consistently done and been up to that point, your faith in him matters immeasurably to the child, and it is that faith that will inevitably carry him through the roughest realities.

Here's the beautiful irony: The more you've invested, the more of yourself you are setting aside when you send them off. (All the time, effort, energy I've put into this child...how can I let him go?) Yet, at the same time, it's all that investment that pays off in the form of trust that your child places in your description of reality and your faith in his capacity to succeed, both of which, of course, are preparation for success and resilience.

> Because of everything that you have consistently done and been up to that point, your faith in him matters immeasurably to the child, and it is that faith that will inevitably carry him through the roughest realities.

If we give into weakness and simply nurse our heartbrokenness in front of our child as he stands poised to venture on his own, we risk sending out a child who is not only worried about whether or not he can face the challenges ahead, but whether or not his parent/teacher will be okay without him.

Daily, in a microcosm, it is dropping your child at school or the school bus stop each morning. There may be a very strong desire to accompany those we love into their daily routines, but that is not our job. And here's a thought: While it is not our job to accompany them, if we pity ourselves, we lose the opportunity to do our actual job at that moment.

As callous as it may sound, we need to *not* feel sorry for our poor selves who have worked so hard to get our kids to this time and our poor selves who are genuinely worried about the kids' welfare and feel entitled to get to share in the joys of discovery in their new "land."

If God would start conducting a therapy session for Moshe, Moshe would not be able to do his job properly for Yehoshua and the Jewish People. We have a really important job that needs to be done right at that moment of our emotional difficulty. Our job is to cease and desist attempts to follow that kid, to coddle him. We need to rise above our own pain and send our kids off faithfully to their next phase; to shift from holding on to letting go with succinct words of warning about what reality is and encouragement of fortitude in the face of that reality.

This is not the time to catch a break or feel sorry for ourselves or them. This is the time to be the adult, and to display compassion in a way that takes into account not just the immediate feelings of people involved, but the possibilities of future circumstances waiting to grow.

Herein lies a broader compassion—a compassion for the future person this child is to become and for circumstances and relationships yet to blossom from this child's impact on the wider world. This kind of compassion rises above the urgency of the moment, beyond time and space, and that's what makes it Godly. God is above time and space. God is the broader picture. To consider the future is one thing; to care about its healthy unfolding is another. And what can be more compassionate than to behave in a manner that facilitates that health?

So there it is—in the pain of letting go, in the discomfort of not coddling, in the seeming callousness of pushing an individual out into a world loaded with risks and unknowns.

And there it has been the whole time: God's compassion.

Contradictions, Faith, and Peace

EIKEV

In Parashat Eikev, Moshe tells the Jews that they will prosper in this world when they fulfill the will of Hashem. One of the rewards promised is, "You will be blessed from all the other nations."[1]

The simple understanding of this verse is that we will receive the most blessings.

Peace (*shalom*) is achieved by the harmonious weaving together of seemingly contradictory circumstances or ideas. What is more contradictory than a merciful God sending suffering, a true God creating falsehood, and a loving God allowing hatred? We are the nation challenged most to pull together seemingly endless contradictions. With what understanding can we pull these contradictions together? With

---

1   *Devarim* 7:14.

the understanding that God is the Source of everything, and there is nothing outside of Him.

The world is contained within God's *sheleimut*, meaning "wholeness." And the glue that binds our basket of *shalom* is *emunah*.

A twenty-year-old yeshiva student had a dying father. The student confidently told his rabbi that he had faith that Hashem would heal his father. The rabbi responded, "Having faith does not mean that Hashem will bring healing. Tragedies happen. Having faith means knowing there is a master plan and hoping that one day we'll understand it. And until we understand, we must strengthen each other."

Although the Torah does promise rewards in our lifetime, the midrash clarifies. The main reward for mitzvah observance is in the World to Come; this world does not contain enough pleasure for sufficient reward.

A story is told of the great Rabbi Pinchas ben Yair. Two merchants left two measures of wheat kernels in Rabbi Pinchas's care. The merchants left town without retrieving their kernels. When sowing time arrived, Rabbi Pinchas planted those kernels. When harvest time arrived, Rabbi Pinchas harvested that grain. He stored that grain in his granary until sowing season arrived again. Then he sowed the kernels from that grain. Seven years later, the merchants returned looking for their property. To the merchants' overwhelming surprise, Rabbi Pinchas showed them the overflowing granaries. "All this grain is yours!" he exclaimed.

Similarly, when we leave our deeds in God's care, He sows and grows them into immeasurably more than we could ever imagine! Through knowing that our perspective is limited, our faith can grow. With faith, we can live with contradictory pieces, and when we weave all those parts together, we become a nation that invites and retains blessing.

Truth Rush

RE'EH

In Southern California, when fifth graders learn American history, they usually take a trip to someplace where they meet actors dressed in mid-1800s garb who are telling tales of hardship and over-coming adversity in an effort to stimulate interest in the historical accounts of the gold rush. The kids get to pan for gold in a makeshift stream with flat metal tins, trying to find the "golden" nuggets, which, of course, are just regular stones that have been spray-painted gold. Each child gets a little brown flax pouch with a drawstring to keep the wealth they accrue.

Recently, our youngest daughter had the opportunity to have that gold rush experience. When she came home with her pouch of gold, it triggered a flashback memory in me.

Here it is: I am eleven years old. I am at Knotts Berry Farm on the gold rush trip with my classmates. I am standing at the stream. I am handed a tin and given instructions to dip it into the water and wave it through gently, hoping to catch some gold stones. I lift the pan and see one gold stone and many regular stones. As I am about to select the

gold one and release the rest, my cynical/realist self stops me. Knowing
I can just color them all gold myself, I think, *Maybe I'll keep all the stones.*
I am about to put them in my pouch. Then I change my mind again, and
I release them all, knowing I can collect any old stones from anywhere
and do the same thing. Then my self-aware self kicks in and I know that
I will not do that, because I'd rather ride my bike, swim with friends, or
read a book than collect and paint stones.

(Sidetrack: During my flashback, a thought occurred to me...

- If I were my younger brother at that time, I'd collect lots of
stones, paint them all, convince friends they were real gold, and
sell the stones out of my third-grade briefcase.
- If I were my older brother, I'd convince my younger brother to
collect and paint and sell them and give me the money for my
seventh-grade needs.)

Back to my memory: I just decide to have fun at the stream, listening
to the instructor just enough to seem interested while making weird
noises and giggling with friends quietly enough so as not to get into
trouble. Then I use the pouch to collect dirt to contribute to a "potion"
that one friend and I would laughingly mix on Sunday in her backyard.

Flash-forward to my adult brain: Panning for gold reminds me of
what we need to do today if we want the real stuff. We need to pan
for truth. We need to sift through information in search of truth. And
there is so much information—information today is like those stones.
Some stones appear to be gold, and we must ask ourselves if the place in
which we are "panning" is set up in such a way that has us fooled.

With this in mind, we owe it to ourselves to at least attempt to pan/
sift in a place that is most objectively offering reality. Sure, we won't
find "golden nuggets" as easily as in the place that's a setup, so we won't
feel a rush of excitement as quickly or as often. The gold/truth we do
find, however, has more of a chance of being the real deal and hence
objectively valuable.

In 2014, while we were living in Cape Town, South Africa, I was brows-
ing through the shelves of a bookstore and I found a small book entitled
How Do You Kill 11 Million People? Before I tell you that I purchased

the book, it may be helpful for you to know that the subtitle was *Why the Truth Matters More Than You Think*. The way the cashier rushed to quickly ring up my purchase, with no eye contact, made me realize she'd probably only glanced at the main title, figured it was a how-to book, and hoped to swiftly get me away from her immediate radius.

Truth matters. The statement is simple enough. Finding truth years ago was less complicated, simply because we had less access to information. I'm not saying it was easier to find truth, just that there was less available to sift through. There were a few news stations on TV, there were magazines, newspapers, books, and the people we could reach in person or by phone. That's it. We can only come to conclusions and make decisions based on the information we already have, and it is delusional (and arrogant) to think that we ever have all the information. We used to give ourselves a reasonable amount of time to research, read, and listen to people who mattered to us. Then, knowing that we'd probably not get much more information, we'd listen to our thoughts and decide on what we believed to be true. And if we were fairly decent people, we'd speak and act in accordance with those truths.

Today is different. Today, we know, there is a continuous flow of information about everything. With this, I must think differently than I used to. I can't honestly say that I probably won't get much more information because I definitely *can* always get more information. The challenge of decision-making today is not in searching for truth but in sifting for truth.

If I simply want the feel-good rush of getting information, I'll pan in the shallow waters at the staged "panning for gold" station. If I want truth, I'll pan in less apparent, un-staged waters...less messed-with—because the purer the source, the more truthful the product

Parashat Re'eh opens mid-chapter with the following words: "[You] See. I give before you today—blessing and curse."[1] It is no coincidence that the Hebrew word for blessing actually means "source." And the

---

1   *Devarim* 13:26.

Hebrew word for curse contains the word "easy." Lies are easy to come by. And half-truths abound.

Rabbi Eliyahu Safran tells a story of a captain and a mate on a ship. A daily log was kept, chronicling life on the ship. One day, the mate uncharacteristically consumed a bit too much alcohol. The captain decided to write in the ship's log, "Mate drunk today."

The captain explained, "This is the fact. The truth is the truth," as if it were his duty to log every truth. The next day was the mate's turn to write in the ship's log. He wrote, "Captain sober today."

Waters of ultimate truth can be muddied with selfish intent. The Source of truth is God. And our objective in life is to be on a path toward God. Falsehood can be identified as information that leads us away from the Source.

The answer to the title question of the book I bought in that Cape Town bookstore (*How Do You Kill 11 Million People?*) was on its opening pages: "Lie to them."

So, I'm thinking, if you can kill that many people by lying to them—which we know has historically happened too many times—you must be able to save people by…telling truth to them. Following this logic, I may at least be able to save myself by telling truth to myself.

If I hope for any salvation, I've got to be willing to think critically, ask courageous questions, sift through all kinds of "truths," and hold those truths up to the tests of context and intent. I've also got to keep traveling to find streams connected to authentic sources, and when I finally find something connected to authenticity, if I can add complimentary thinking to my critical thinking, I can stay connected to truth and become a stream or a tributary or a delta of truth.

Then if some kids come panning for truth from me, they might actually strike some gold, even if they are also quietly making weird noises and giggling and hoping I won't hear.

What's In, What's Up

SHOFTIM

Above the kitchen counter in one of our married children's homes hangs a quote attributed to Rabbi Shimshon Raphael Hirsch:

> If man cannot bring into his home the same spirit that he propounds in the outside world, then his work is worthless. If he does not conduct his home life with the same dedication to truth, reverence of heaven and belief for which he fights and pours out his heart-blood outside the home, then his efforts are in vain. He would be better setting down his torch if he cannot open his home to the world and say: Here, look and see if there is any contradiction with which I preach to the world.

Parashat Shoftim includes the mitzvot that apply to a king. One of the mitzvot is for a king to write his own Torah. The Hebrew wording, *"mishneh haTorah*—a copy of the Torah,"[1] prompts *Rashi* to explain that

---

1   *Devarim* 17:18.

the king actually writes two Torah scrolls: one that stays in his treasury and one that he keeps with him at all times.

The text is explicit about what to do with the latter: "It shall be with him, and he shall read from it all the days of his life, so that he will learn to fear Hashem, his God, to observe all the words of this Torah and these decrees, to perform them, so that his heart does not become haughty over his brothers and does not turn from the mitzvot right or left."[2] This Torah is a personal guide to life for the leader to live as an exemplary citizen.

The Torah is teaching us that people in leadership positions are expected to study more often, to develop more *yirat Hashem* (awe of God), to perform more mitzvot, to be more humble, to be more particular in all areas of character and observance than those who look to them for guidance.

When we apply this to our lives, we can go from macro to micro. We are always leaders of those with less life experience. Teachers are leaders of their students; parents are leaders of their children; and we are each leaders of ourselves—the stronger part of ourselves leads the weaker aspects.

> We are always leaders of those with less life experience. Teachers are leaders of their students; parents are leaders of their children; and we are each leaders of ourselves—the stronger part of ourselves leads the weaker aspects.

We call the Torah *"Torat Chayim"* because it is living and life-giving, so the Torah that accompanies the king as he goes about his life would seem to demonstrate this clearly enough. So what is the idea of keeping a Torah in the treasury? What is the purpose of an unused Torah?

I think we would each do well to own two Torahs, so to speak. Ideally, Torah should be that which we both draw from and simply cherish. The Torah that we draw from, we schlep around with us, which inevitably

---

2   Ibid., 17:19–20.

means there's a risk of mishandling, misinterpreting, or misapplying it. Because whenever we use something, there is risk of misuse.

The Torah that remains in the treasure house reminds the leader that there is an untouchable aspect of Torah, and this makes it prized so that even if we would not live by the Torah, Torah remains valuable. We cherish Torah not just because of what we get from it, but because it is the word of God.

I venture to say there is a spectrum from Treasure House Torah to Traveling Torah:

- Treasure House Torah—the sacred word of God is simply cherished, protected, and tucked away—"I protect Torah."
- Traveling Torah—the sacred words are used for intellectual debate and practical application—"I live Torah."

The pitfall of the former is that Torah is so holy, so ideal, it is separate from me. The pitfall of the latter is that Torah is so close, always available, I may twist its teachings to fit with or justify my lower self. My view of God will affect where I am on the spectrum. Do I think of God as separate from me? Or do I think that personal conscience is also part of God (in the form of my soul)?

When we know that God lives in us and beyond us and we know that Torah is God's word, we can understand the idea of the "untouchable" Torah and the "experiential" Torah.

We can come to both protect the sacredness of Torah and still practically utilize it.

Seeds of Giving

KI TEITZEI

My husband bought a bird feeder. This was challenging for me, not because I am against feeding birds; I am against owning unnecessary paraphernalia.

He assembled it and gingerly hung it just outside the kitchen window. The kids were excited! The birds were not. The birds didn't seem to know that this was the all-you-can-eat best deal in town. Not even one fine feathered friend so much as circled curiously.

The five-year-old suggested that we put up a big sign so the birds would know what was on offer here. "Birds Eat Free!"

Do the birds need us hanging seeds out for them? Which bird asked for this? In *Parashat Ki Teitzei*, God tells us of two nations whose men are not accepted as Jews for a few generations after the Exodus from Egypt, one of which was Ammon. Why were the men of Ammon not allowed into the congregation of Israel? What unspeakable crime had they committed that none of their men may be admitted into the ranks of Judaism?

Get this: The Ammonites did not offer sustenance to the Jews who were passing by the land of Ammon during their travels in the wilderness.

What? C'mon, that's it? No man from Ammon could be a Jew because when the Jews were passing by (clearly, by the way, already being taken care of by God), no Ammonite man ventured out of the city to look for passersby and offer food and water. That's grounds for one's descendants not being accepted as converts? Seriously?

Seriously.

We recently read about a detailed procedure called *"eglah arufah,"* in which many important members of the community get involved in being excused for the unexplained death of a passing traveler. Though no one suspects any of those leaders of the actual murder, great pains are taken to remind the community that the root of the possibility of murder is insensitivity to the value of life. To exonerate themselves from the possibility of being the (indirect) cause of the crime, the leaders must declare that they never sent anyone away from their town unaccompanied or without provisions for the way. Those are acts of giving that support the claim of being sensitive to the value of life.

When we go out of our way to care for the physical needs of others, we show that each life is precious, and we are being Godly. Hashem provides for each individual, but still, He does not want us to use that fact as an excuse not to care for others but rather as an example of what we can strive to do in order to be closer to Godliness. That the men of the nation of Ammon did not offer provisions was representative of their overall "can't be bothered" attitude. They were not concerned with anybody else. The fact is, not one person from the entire nation came out of his home to give something, anything, to the passersby. They had no drive to give, and they did not give. The nation that breeds indifference to the needs of others will not rise to the challenge of representing God in this world.

Back to the birds: Those birds need us to put seeds out like the traveling Jews needed food and water from Ammon. So what's the point of offering? The point is that we become givers when we give, regardless of whether or not the others need it.

Yes, there is a deeper level of giving that is about assessing the needs of the receiver. This is integral to building a relationship. Still, there is a basic level of giving that is just about the giver. It's about making the concept of valuing another human being become and remain a part of our psyches. It's why we teach our children to bring gifts to friends who host them. It's why it's better to give a dollar a day to charity for a hundred days than one hundred dollars every hundred days. The more acts of giving, the more we become givers. And God wants a nation and a world of active givers.

I'm beginning to think that this bird feeder is quite useful, inasmuch as it can serve as a reminder of the importance of simply giving because we want to be Godly. So it's great that the kids are excited.

When I tell my husband that the five-year-old thinks we should hang a sign for the birds, he tells her he thinks it's a good idea. She folds her arms, rolls her eyes, and says with not just a bit of condescension, "And Imma (Mom) thinks that birds can't read."

Possession Is Not Nine–Tenths

KI TAVO

When my younger brothers were little and they wanted to give a gift to our parents, they would find something that they considered their own. They'd wrap it up and give it with high hopes for connection and appreciation. I recall my parents receiving interesting birthday gifts: Matchbox cars without wheels, a scratched Tonka truck, a few Tinker toys or Lincoln Logs. Sometimes, gifts would be presented in some kind of makeshift wrapping—a tissue, a leaf, a Fruit of the Loom undershirt.

My parents would receive these offerings with great respect and sensitivity to the young 'uns, even though they certainly could have taken the opportunity to make it clear to the child that the thimble from the Monopoly game was not really theirs to give.

In *Parashat Ki Tavo*, the Jew is commanded to "take" from the *bikkurim*, the "first fruits" Hashem has given, and offer that food to…Hashem.

Hashem, the Source of all, would "receive" the first fruits through the Kohanim in the Beit Hamikdash. The general understanding of the purpose for bringing *bikkurim* is, foremost, so that we, like my little brothers, become givers, and even better—grateful givers.

I'd like to suggest that the giving of *bikkurim* could also help us to become ideal receivers. Here's how: When we are the ones giving, we can notice what we would like from the receiver. Then we can put those hopes into practice when the tables are turned. Ideal receivers receive not just the gift, but the giver. Ideal receivers do not focus exclusively on the item being given; they focus on who the giver is to them. They focus on the meaning of the gift-giving for the relationship. An ideal receiver appreciates the giver through the gift.

It is interesting to notice that in the same verse that we find the mitzvah to bring the *bikkurim*, we are told: "Put it in a *teneh*." The Hebrew word *teneh* is easily translated as "basket." Traditionally, wealthy people brought the *bikkurim* on expensive trays, which they took back home with them. Poorer people brought *bikkurim* in handmade wicker or straw baskets, which the Kohanim kept. While the expensive trays were obtained with minimal effort from the giver, those handmade baskets had the poor people's efforts in them. Hence, we might think it seems kinder to return the basket that the poor man invested time, energy, thought, and heart into. However, the fact that the Kohen kept the poor man's basket is a lesson to us. It is kinder to fully embrace a simple, heartfelt offering in the service of the One Who gives time, energy, thought, and emotion than to focus on the poverty of the giver by rejecting some of his offering.

Personal application: How good of a receiver am I?

- Do I gratefully acknowledge small gifts (compliments, thank-yous) that are offered as means of connection?
- Do I recognize what might be more of an effort for one who is poorer in a particular area and cherish those efforts as valuable "wrapping"?

Possession, in reality, is an illusion. It is a necessary illusion for the healthy functioning of society. And it is a helpful illusion in that we get to become givers and receivers in Godly ways.

Our Turn

NITZAVIM

We are told to "choose life!"[1] Why? "So that you will live, you and your children!"[2]

Isn't that sort of like saying, "Choose food, so you will eat"? Clearly, there is a deeper meaning to the word "live" than simply having a pulse. The next verse can add a deeper dimension to our understanding. For what will you live? "To love Hashem your God, to listen to His voice and to cleave to Him."

Okay, this offers a focus. Love, listen, cleave. I suppose I can listen to God by following a path of *mesorah* passed through generations, and perhaps I am cleaving to Him by emulating His traits. Yet love is mentioned first, so, practically, how do I reach the goal of loving Hashem?

Rabbi Eliyahu Dessler tells me that giving leads to love. What can I give to God, since God doesn't really need anything I have to offer? While it's true that God does not need us to give Him anything, He does accept

---

1   *Devarim* 30:19.
2   Ibid.

our attention. I believe that we can come to love Hashem by paying attention to His presence in the world. In this way we are "giving" something to Hashem—we are giving Him our attention. He is accepting of this, and because we are giving Him something, we come to love Him.

John Gottman, PhD, studies married couples' behavior. He found that most spouses who physically turn to face one another during small interactions have lasting marriages. Regularly facing the one you are addressing or the one who addresses you means you are giving them your attention. Couples who do not show that they can pay attention to each other for small stuff often find it difficult to face each other for the big stuff, and for the important stuff they turn away. Then the niggling discomfort that the spouse is disinterested can become the pain of disconnection. Turning away is easy, noncommittal, nonconfrontational—and non-bonding.

> Most spouses who physically turn to face one another for small interactions have lasting marriages.

The good news is that turning toward another is behavioral. By simply focusing on the action of facing another, the dynamic of the relationship changes. You are opening the door to a lasting relationship.

How do I love Hashem? *"Kaveh el Hashem."*[3] Turn to Him, turn away from distractions, and pay attention. If we want to choose life, we are signing up to love Hashem, and in order to love Hashem, we need to give Him something He will accept.

He will accept our attention and interest in Him.

So let's turn toward Him.

---

3   *Tehillim* 27:14.

How to Not Be Evil

VAYEILECH

Consider the end of the Torah, recounting Moshe's last day on earth: the seventh day of the twelfth month (Adar), in the year 2488 from Creation.

Moshe writes a Torah scroll and teaches Torah to Yehoshua, the Kohanim, and all the people. As Moshe commands the Kohanim to place the Torah scroll beside the *Aron* (Ark of the Covenant), we might think that Moshe will reiterate to the people the necessary centrality of Torah living. Instead, though, the people get what sounds like an earful of rebuke: "For I know your rebelliousness and your stiff neck! Behold, during my lifetime you have been rebels against God and still that will be after my death."

Two verses later, he expounds: "For I know after my death you will surely act corruptly. You will stray from the path I have commanded you." What is Moshe hoping to accomplish by telling the people that they will behave badly?

To understand what benefit there might be in this, let's make it personal: How is it helpful for me to know that I will do terrible things?

Here's what I think: If I live in denial of my dark side, I am in grave danger of not noticing when it knocks on the door of my consciousness or rears its ugly head in my interactions. If I live in denial of the inevitability of my rebelliousness, I miss out on the capacity to prevent or respond to my rebelliousness. In such a state, I will be susceptible to being completely wrong or off in my assessments of reality and behavior. Then I open myself to developing narcissistic patterns of casting off burdens of accountability. In that slippery slope, I could become a master of shame and blame and manipulation to twist the reality of my own wrongdoing into perverted versions of the stories in which I am the victim of circumstance and ill intentions of others. This is a psychological black hole I'd like to avoid.

Canadian professor and psychotherapist Jordan Peterson studied how decent people have historically come to do indecent things. A book he recommends called *Ordinary Men* outlines how ordinary citizens could come to commit atrocities. Peterson tells his university students that they absolutely would have joined the Nazi party if they had been living at that time. To think that we are somehow above or better than that behavior is self-deluding.

The idea is that until we accept that we have the capacity to carry out acts of evil, we will be susceptible to doing just that! The more I know about how I can and will mess up, the more I can work to prevent myself from being a total disaster. I can also develop a self-consciousness that will bring my rebellious behavior to my attention (ta-da!), and, even better, I will notice my thoughts that could lead to such behavior. In this way, I can minimize the damage to myself and others.

Additionally, if I know I will mess up, I can humbly preplan the strategy to make amends so I'll be able to make those amends more expediently after each misstep, without time spent digging through ego and arrogance. Although we might think it's better for people in leadership positions to just remind us of our successes, stroke our fragile egos, and tell us, "You are *amazing* and *awesome*" and "You are totally perfect the way you are, and anybody who doesn't see that is a loser," the Torah's lesson here cannot be overstated: We must know that we are not unquestionably awesome. In fact, we each carry an immeasurable capacity for evil.

While *Merriam-Webster* defines evil as "morally reprehensible," I hesitate to accept that definition. This is because cultural definitions of morality are varied. In our own times, what was once deemed infanticide and would certainly have fit into the category of "morally reprehensible" is being renamed late-term abortion. All sorts of pleasure-seeking practices and confusing living arrangements are protected from criticism in the Bubble Wrap of "tolerance."

In Torah life, *tov*, "good," means alignment with Godliness, while *ra*, "evil," works toward disconnection from Godliness.

In Peterson's 2013 talk on "Tragedy and Evil," he defines evil as "the conscious attempt to make the conditions of existence more pathological." This definition resonates with me, because it assumes that evil is not something external to man; it is perpetrated by human beings. This idea is in harmony with the Torah concept of *yetzer hara*—the inclination toward pathology that lives in us. Peterson's definition also reminds us that personal accountability looms large: The person involved in the evil is still accountable, even if the end looks good.

We have all seen "good" things evolve from evil behavior. Results are God's domain, but efforts are ours. While we can argue about depth of evil based on depth of consciousness, it is reasonable to think that when an individual is involved in manipulative planning toward causing disconnect, this is evidence of conscious attempts, and this is behavior to avoid.

Back to Moshe on his last day, telling the people, "You will be rebellious. You will stray." Imagine we are hearing Moshe saying this to us. What would we be thinking? What would we be feeling? Here's how I imagine the thought/feeling journey to go:

Thought: *If you are telling us this, Moshe, it must be true.*

Feeling: Despair

Thought: *If you are telling all of us, it's not just me; I'm not alone.*

Feeling: Connected

Thought: *If you are telling us, it must be that there is something we can do about it.*

Feeling: Hope

Thought: *There must be things that we, our children, and all future generations can do!*

Feeling: Determination

Thought: *We can make plans to live in ways that will keep us far from evil. We can continuously make good choices and keep learning Torah from valid sources and check ourselves to be sure we stand far from rebelliousness against Godliness. Then, when we do wrong, we'll recognize it and mindfully redirect ourselves back toward goodness.*

So...it's a good thing that Moshe told it straight. We should expect nothing less from leaders who know their own capacity for evil and who love us enough to want us to know ours.

Now, *that* is awesome.

Raising Elders

HAAZINU

Today, I was told in no uncertain terms by one of my just-turned-teen children that the last thing I ever did for her was give birth to her. I burst out laughing. And my child was left wondering what it was that I found so amusing. She insisted that the whole reason I had children was so that they could be my slaves.

To offer some context, we had just arrived home from grocery shopping, and I had asked her to carry a few bags from the trunk of the car into the house and to put away those groceries. Of course, there is always more context, and, of course, she did bring in the groceries and put them away, albeit with some dramatic tween foot-dragging.

That evening, through my laughter, I told my husband the child's line about me not doing anything for her since birth. As I repeated the ridiculous claim, I realized that one of the reasons I did not actually take any offense to the claim was because I had immediately pictured the child's older siblings rebuking her. I knew that if any one of the older children had been in the car, they would have, each in his or her own way, shut down that idea. They would have said something like, "Kid, you have no idea what you're talking about. Anything you have and get to do is because Imma and Abba provide for your needs, and they give you opportunities and teach and guide you. Say you're sorry to Imma, now!" Then if it was a brother, he might pick her up and jokingly threaten to put her into the garbage bin if she didn't apologize.

What does any of this have to do with *Parashat Haazinu*? *Haazinu* is a poem/song about how Hashem is just, yet we, His children, will stray. Then disease and enemies will ravage the Jewish People, and it will only be Hashem's mercy that will save us from complete destruction. Early in the song, the Jewish People are told: "Remember the days of yore, understand generation after generation. Ask your father and he will tell you; your elders and they will tell you."[1]

I wonder why the text says to ask both your elders and your father? Why not just ask your father? Or just ask your elders? The root of the Hebrew word for father is *av*, which means foundation. The best way to live our lives is to live by unchanging core values. In striving to live by the same solid foundation that has stood the test of time, we can remember and understand the past by "asking" that foundation. If we hope to not be bogged down by the challenges of the present moment, it is helpful to look for guidance from that foundation, which is beyond time.

The wording of that verse enlightens me. For guidance from core values, I must seek and ask. Yet for guidance from elders, the verse says "they will tell you," which seems to suggest that the elders will tell you even if you don't ask. What comes to mind initially are those old people who are regularly dispensing unsolicited advice, but I'm thinking that an elder is anyone who's "been there." As I write this, our oldest child is thirty and our youngest is thirteen. The older children can be elders to the younger, especially once the "elders" have their own children. They've "been there."

Although on the surface the verse is intended to be an instruction to the younger generations, I find it to be a comfort to the older generation to know that if we are blessed to live long enough to be considered elders,

---

1   *Devarim* 32:7.

we will not be alone in telling the truth. We will be joined by the elders of the next generation, to the point that they will even speak for us.

And sometimes, just the knowledge that they will speak for us is enough to hearten us and keep us from getting in the way of the growth of the next elders-to-be.

Teaching Backward, Reaching Up

V'ZOT HABERACHAH

Among the many challenges he has undertaken, in the late 1970s, as principal of a Jewish day school, my father taught American history to high schoolers. Rumor has it, Dr. Lerner would stand on his desk to capture and keep the attention of his students while introducing a lesson. My father would also "teach backward." This does not mean that my father turned his back on the students. Rather, he would begin the school year teaching recent history, and as the year progressed, he would guide the students further back into earlier history.

The Talmud enjoins every father to teach verses of the Torah to his young child who is just beginning to speak.[1] The *Shulchan Aruch* (the code of Jewish law) categorizes this Talmudic teaching as an obligation based on the Torah teaching, "*V'limadetem otam et beneichem l'daber*

---

1   *Sukkah* 42a.

bam—And you shall teach them, your children, to speak in it."[2] The *Shulchan Aruch* goes on to say that the first verse a child should be taught is "*Torah tzivah lanu Moshe morashah kehillat Yaakov*—Moshe commanded us Torah, an inheritance of the congregation of Yaakov,"[3] which is found in *Parashat V'zot Haberachah*.

The second verse the Sages say to teach our children is "*Shema Yisrael Hashem Elokeinu Hashem Echad*—Hear [nation of] Israel, Hashem is our God. Hashem is One."[4]

Wait. That's the second verse to teach a child? Not the first? The declaration of *Shema* is the bedrock of our faith. We say *Shema* in our daily prayers and before retiring at night. The words of *Shema* are meant to be the last words a Jew says before death. Shouldn't we first teach a child the most accepted declaration of our faith? Shouldn't the fact of Torah being commanded to us by Moshe be secondary to the fact of the Oneness of Hashem? So why do we teach a young child about Torah from Moshe first?

I'd like to suggest that a person needs to first experience human connection before he can receive the concept of Hashem's oneness. A child who does not feel connected to his family will struggle to sense the reality of the reality that all the universe, time, and space are interconnected through God.

The words of the first verse to teach a child are about Hashem's Torah, through people—Moshe and Yaakov. Moshe is the human connection between us and God, an ideal for us to learn how to relate to Hashem through Torah. And Yaakov is the first of our fathers from whom only the Jewish People descend; the first man whom no other nation can claim as their father. So to a child, there is this great man Moshe, the first leader of our people who received a message for all Jews—Yaakov's children—for all time. The verse of *Torah Tzivah* is initially more relatable than *Shema*.

---

2   *Yoreh Deah* 245:5.
3   *Devarim* 33:4.
4   Ibid., 6:4.

226 Up to God

Then it's time for the second verse: "Hear, Yisrael [i.e., the name of the more developed Yaakov], Hashem is our God. Hashem is One." And when the child wonders, "Who is Hashem?" we can say, "Hashem is the One Who gave the Torah to Moshe. And you already know Moshe, that great man who brought us the Torah as an inheritance for the family of Yaakov."

And the child thinks, *Oh yeah, I know Moshe. He's the one who got the Torah for me and my family.* After establishing that, the connection to Hashem can grow. And so it seems that the value of teaching backward goes way back.

Following this line of thinking, if I am experiencing difficulty connecting to Hashem as my God or as One, what can I do? I can find the point of connection through a person I know who is connected. I can remind myself that this intelligent, thinking, kind person knows Hashem enough to keep incorporating *Torat Moshe* into her life. That personal connection can be an impetus to expand my mind "back" to Hashem. While we may think of *mesorah*, the chain of Jewish tradition, as starting with Moshe and being passed down to us, it is helpful to visualize the *mesorah* the other way: from me, reaching back to Moshe at Sinai.

And while I'm at it, I can imagine Moshe standing high on Har Sinai. For that visualization I can begin by picturing someone I know well. Standing on his desk.

The Blessed Defense

V'ZOT HABERACHAH

"And this is the blessing with which Moshe, man of God, blessed the children of Israel before he died."

Why is Moshe described here as "ish ha'Elokim—man of God"?

Pesikta D'Rav Kahana, a collection of midrash compiled in the late 1800s, says the term "man of God" is reserved for a person who speaks in defense of the Jewish People. Rav Avraham Saba, a late 1400s Spanish scholar, writes that Moshe was called "man of God" here because he acted like God by forgiving the sins of the Jews and blessing them—as God does.

We know that classic commentators can have different opinions that can all be true. So let's say Moshe was both forgiving the people and defending them before he blessed them. What is it the commentators think that Moshe needed to forgive or defend? And why could Moshe not simply have been blessing the people before he died?

To understand this, we can wonder why might it have been difficult for Moshe to bless the people before he died. Well, the last verse in the previous Torah portion reads as follows: "And you [Moshe] will not go

227

into the Land that I gave the children of Israel." Okay, we know that Moshe desperately desired to enter Israel, and we have various understandings of why Hashem did not allow Moshe into the Land. Back in *Parashat Va'etchanan*, Moshe was speaking to the Jewish People when he said, "Hashem was angry at me because of you, and He [Hashem] would not listen to me."[1] It seems that Moshe was blaming the people for Hashem's decision to forbid him to enter the Promised Land.

When we do not get what we want, it is certainly human to resent the people we think got in the way of our dreams. From the verse in *Parashat Va'etchanan*, it seems Moshe's human nature is on display. Yet Moshe, being Godly, does not leave it at that. In this *parashah*, Moshe shows that he has moved past his human nature, knowing that the end goal is not just to accept his fate, or even just to forgive the people, but to wholeheartedly bless the people.

With this awareness, we can understand why Moshe would want to be at the point of defending (i.e., explaining the behavior of) the people. For then he could know that he had fully forgiven the people and his blessing could be *b'lev shalem*—wholehearted.

I certainly do not claim to know through what process Moshe became a "man of God." I do, though, know that it is much more difficult to be a "man of God" amid people than alone. Moshe certainly was already Godly amid his flock of sheep in Midyan before Hashem pushed him to be the leader of the most stubborn people!

We can relate, because we know that our most difficult struggles on the road to being Godly involve other people. So we need a process, a plan, some kind of way to move to a place of wholeheartedly blessing someone whose actions and words have played a role in hurting us.

(Crucial caveat: The Jewish People were not purposely attempting to shut Moshe off from his dream of entering the Promised Land. They were simply displaying human selfishness, as most of us do, and their selfishness played a role in Moshe's fate. The following formula is for regular use regarding normal people in our lives. I do still believe the

---

1   *Devarim* 3:26.

formula can be used regarding a person who displays patterns of malicious behavior—even without substantial signs of remorse and change. However, in those cases, it definitely takes extraordinary mental and emotional efforts and, most critically, continuous boundary enforcement. Without enforcing boundaries—what is okay and what is not okay for others to say/do to me—you are continuously inviting that personality to hurt you, which leads you to resent yourself, and which will take another process to undo.)

Here's a formula for thought and striving that can lead from resentment to blessing:

> I know that I feel hurt by the speech/actions of that person.
> I know that I am far from perfect.
> I know that Hashem runs the world.
> I know that the one I blamed did the best he could with what he had at that time.
> I will strive to recognize the gap between my expectations and reality.
> I will be open to the discomfort I experience when I sit in that gap.
> I will strive to close that gap in a healthy way, with that which is in my circle of control.
> I will strive to regularly identify real goodness that I admire in that person.
> I will strive to appreciate goodness that results from knowing that person.
> I will strive to be prepared to defend that person in the face of accusations (mine included).
> I will strive to wholeheartedly bless that person, that is, to cultivate in myself a hope and desire for Godly experiences to flow toward, through, and from them.

I can choose to seek, develop, and utilize processes that help me to move past resentments toward becoming a staunch forgiver, defender, and blesser of others. It is my hope that my aspirations and efforts toward being a "person of God" will stand in my much-needed defense and as blessings for me along my way and at my end.

FESTIVALS

FESTIVALS

Heads I Win

ROSH HASHANAH

"Heads I win, tails you lose." It was my older brother's sneaky way of ensuring his status as the coin-flipping champion when we were kids.

"And Hashem will make you the head and not the tail."[1] On Rosh Hashanah, we ask that we be granted this blessing. Before we understand this blessing, it is good to know that the purpose of Rosh Hashanah is to give us the opportunity to proclaim Hashem as our King.

So:

1. How is this blessing connected to the purpose of the day?
2. Is this blessing about each of us being a leader?
3. If yes to number 2, what about, "Better to be the tail of a lion than the head of a fox"?[2]

---

1   *Devarim* 28:13.
2   *Pirkei Avot* 4:20.

234 Up to God

To answer the last question first, here we are enjoined to follow those headed toward goodness rather than lead people away from goodness. Fine. So the blessing could be, "May you follow the right path and proclaim God as King! Amen!"

To know why my made-up blessing doesn't make the grade as a Rosh Hashanah blessing, I need to understand the meaning of the real Rosh Hashanah blessing. Rabbi Shimshon Pincus mentions the idea that at the end of a lifetime of Torah learning, a man may find himself being referred to as "the tail, because his soul was not satiated." How could a soul still be hungry after years of feasting on Torah study?

Sadly, there is a way—if the man's actions were simply "because everyone in my community is doing it." The same lifetime of study could have satiated his soul had he used his own mind to decide that the reason for his learning was to align himself as much as possible with God. That others are doing the same is a fringe benefit—it's wonderful and even imperative to have a support system to inspire and uplift us along the way of doing good—but fitting in should not be the sole motivating reason for learning Torah.

To answer the second question: Yes! We each need to be leaders. We need to lead ourselves! We need to be "a head of ourselves." On Rosh Hashanah, I ask that Hashem kick-start me to the level of leading myself even as I follow the path that others have paved before me and others are following today.

Nobody else can recognize for me that Hashem is the Sovereign. I need to do that for myself.

Keeping in mind the purpose of Rosh Hashanah brings us to the answer of the first question: Nobody else can recognize for me that Hashem is the Sovereign. I need to do that for myself.

I cannot possibly succeed in the mission of Rosh Hashanah—proclaiming God as my king—unless I am "a head and not a tail." With this perspective, the fact that we say this blessing on Rosh Hashanah makes perfect sense.

Rabbi Menachem Mendel Schneerson once listened to a man complain that a blessing he had been given had not come to fruition. The

Rebbe explained that blessings are like rain for a farmer's field: If the farmer tilled and plowed and planted, then the rain will bring forth results. When a person prepares himself, blessings will effect change.

How do I prepare myself to be the recipient of the "head, not tail" blessing? I need to plant seeds. I have to want to be aware of my personal motivations and possibly misleading motivations. I have to open and reopen myself to the reality that Hashem is the Origin and Sustainer of all. In His infinite wisdom, He created all of us and each of us with a plan for us to enjoy the greatest lasting pleasure by following His instructions within our circumstances and abilities.

I may find that I already possess some, if not all, of these understandings, or I may decide that research or review is in order. The energy I put toward reaching those understandings will be my plowed, sown field awaiting the rainfall. The sublime difference between "just following the rules" and "following the rules with appreciation for the Rulemaker's relationship to us" cannot be overstated! It is a difference that will only be known to the follower and God. It is the difference between heads and tails.

Yet unlike the coin-flip deal, because Hashem is infinite, we can all be winners.

In God's Direction

ROSH HASHANAH

We often make use of a service and don't give a moment's thought to its originators, until something changes. Then we say, "Hey, what's going on? This is not the platform I know and got used to. What did 'they' do?"

Most of us don't like change. Change means I'll have to make new efforts. New efforts initially entail learning, and learning is best done with humility. If I am too attached to the feeling of comfort in already knowing, I may not humble myself enough to embrace change. But if I can cherish the value of growth and even anticipate the surprise of what lies ahead, I can at least accept change with amusement and at best invite its power into my life.

There's a message in this whole change thing: How many of us take the time to appreciate Hashem in each day, to recognize Him as the Creator and ultimate Ruler of our whole world? We get on with our lives, using His world every moment. Then something happens that upsets our routine, that makes us stop to figure out how to navigate now that things are different:

- Some people will stage a protest—"I'm against God because He makes life difficult"—without addressing the One in charge.
- Some people will complain loudly, "I hate the way this change makes me feel," also without addressing Him directly.
- Some will simply deny that there is Someone in charge: "Stuff happens." (Those people have no valid excuse for ever being upset, but that's another discussion.)

But some individuals will know there is purpose in each change even if they do not understand the considerations of God. These people will struggle too. They'll feel as disoriented as the others, but they'll say to God directly, "This is so hard! I really don't think I need this now. I mean, I know if You gave it to me then ultimately I do need it, but it's hard for me to accept that idea now, here, today." These individuals will allow themselves to feel their God-given feelings and continue communicating directly to the One in charge—the Creator and Supervisor of the whole program, the whole service.

And the great thing is that Hashem not only created the world, He created each of us within His world, and He invites us to be directly connected to Him.

This is one of the opportunities inherent in Rosh Hashanah. We can recognize Hashem as the Creator and King of the world, the One Who is beyond human understanding of time and space, yet so with me that I can address Him directly with all the emotion and intellect He has given me. As circumstances shift and we experience disorientation, it helps to know it's all part of the plan of the Service Provider.

Between Us

YOM KIPPUR

Ten days of repentance, Rosh Hashanah through Yom Kippur.

On Rosh Hashanah, we proclaim God as King. He rules exclusively. He is the only One, and everything that happens is by His Will, not mine.

Ten days later is Yom Kippur—Yom Hakippurim, Day of Atonements, when we atone, making right our wrongdoings. We apologize and ask forgiveness for our insensitivities to and rebellions against the King, the Judge, the only One with all the information to be the Judge. For ten days we say *HaMelech HaMishpat*: God is *the* Judge, the only Judge, the One who can judge us in all fairness. He is the only One who knows our circumstances, struggles, strengths, and limits.

The order of these acceptances is no coincidence. It is after we have an understanding that all we accomplish is through Hashem's beneficence that we obtain a level of humility enough to look honestly at our shortcomings and hold back from judging others. While God will forgive my slights against Him, He expects us to approach each other for forgiveness regarding person-to-person interactions. He does not allow it to be His place to forgive our interpersonal misdemeanors. He leaves that to us to work out, which means He has faith in our abilities to confront ourselves honestly and face each other with a desire to reconnect.

Finding the strength of character within ourselves to ask forgiveness of others takes great humility. It is a humility born of the knowledge that I do not run the world, and I am not the Judge, yet I am important enough that my deeds matter.

Where to start with the forgiveness thing? The measure of a man is in how he treats those closest to him. The point for all of us? Begin at home.

Where We Reside

SUKKOT

What was I supposed to do in South Africa with my *Mizrach* painting?

I unpacked the beautiful painting of the Kotel, the remaining wall of the courtyard of the Beit Hamikdash, with the Hebrew word *mizrach*, "east," fashioned across the top. East is the direction of Yerushalayim, the direction to face during prescribed prayer…from America. But I was then in South Africa…

- Where I drive on the left side of the road (stay left…stay left…), steering from the right side of the car (after first getting into the passenger seat and wondering why there was no steering wheel)
- Where I buy electricity from a store and watch out for electricity thieves(?!)
- Where my house phone searches for a signal, decides it can't find one, and gives up
- Where north is the new east

So I wondered where to hang the *Mizrach* painting. In this world, it makes sense to hang a sign that says "East" on an east-facing wall. However:

- If I hang it on the eastern wall of my home, it will indicate direction and lose its meaning.
- If I hang it on the northern wall, facing Israel, I am aligning the picture with its meaning, yet misleading the direction seekers of "this world" direction.

Still, "this world" directions are temporary. Rabbeinu Bachya, great scholar of the mid 1300s, tells us that our ancestors knew that the sukkot were reminders that all dwellings would be temporary on the road to the Land of Israel. Once in their own land, and even more so with the Beit Hamikdash, they would experience a sense of permanence. Our own sukkah is meant to remind us that all is temporary except the ultimate Infinite One.

The festival of Sukkot is called *Zeman Simchateinu*, "time of our happiness." About what are we happy? We are rejoicing in our vulnerability with the recognition that we are in God's hands, and He is the only true permanence.

Years ago, our four-year-old son reassured us, "In the sukkah, Hashem protects us from the elephants." Clearly, he was confusing elephants with elements. A statement that seemed absolutely incorrect at the time and place, however, seemed somewhat correct later on when we lived in South Africa.

In other words, on some days he might be right, which can sometimes be left. While east can sometimes be north.

Faith and Secure

SUKKOT

Why do we sit in the sukkah? The Talmud discusses two reasons, both of which are true. In the desert, after we left Egypt:

- Jews built huts in the desert.
- God's protective clouds surrounded the Jews in the desert.

If Judaism is about keeping the memory of an ancient heritage alive, then the festival is just a time of commemoration, and the information about the huts suffices. But we need some insight here because Judaism is an eternally applicable way of life. It is God's recipe for individual, national, and global fulfillment. I want to connect to the timeless message of those ancient huts and understand the purpose of those desert clouds.

The Jews built temporary homes under circumstances of undeniable recognition that everything in their possession was from and for Hashem. Although we may not live with the same absolute faith, it is certainly honorable to strive to build our homes with that understanding. We do not live without homes and possessions. We don't pretend that we are angels without basic material needs. Rather, we accept and utilize the gifts of our own abilities, strengths, and resourcefulness to provide shelter for ourselves. This seems a good enough message of the sukkah: Keep a clear awareness that Hashem is the source of everything, even as you care for your own needs.

So why the clouds? What is the added benefit of understanding that my sukkah also represents the *Ananei Ha'kavod*, "Clouds of Glory," which were a manifestation of God's presence in a physical form? The Jews who built their desert booths were witness to the plagues in Egypt. They experienced the awesome splitting of the sea. They knew God from Sinai. They had *mann* falling from the sky, and a well of pure drinking water flowing through the camp every day. They had Moshe Rabbeinu as their leader, for His sake. Did they really need another constant visual reminder of God? Could they possibly forget that God was with them? Certainly not.

Yet maybe they could forget something else. Something about which they needed reassurance: Perhaps they could forget that Hashem is the Protector.

The *Ananei Ha'kavod* were a constant sign of Hashem's protection. Sure, Hashem could have protected them without the clouds, and we may think these people should not have needed a sign of protection. Yet the clouds were there. We might think, *If only God would surround us with those clouds today, we would be so faithful!* But God doesn't provide those clouds for us, and that means we don't need them.

And that generation did need them? Yes! Theirs was an entire generation that knew firsthand what it was to feel neglected and rejected. They lived through unrelenting persecution in Egypt for their entire lives prior to witnessing the miraculous salvation. They were born into lives of pain and despair that could be traced back two hundred years! The fear of feeling unprotected may understandably have haunted them. So the generation with every reason to have faith in God was also the one with every reason to fear that God would leave them vulnerable.

That we are invited to connect to the sukkah both as a booth and as the clouds reveals a key understanding about closeness to God in various eras. We may be tempted to dwell on differences between us and the generation that wandered under God's direct providence, to disassociate ourselves from their level of closeness to Hashem and to say, "That was then; this is now. We can't possibly be that close."

And so we get caught in the commemoration trap, and we miss tapping into the deep power of the festival. Because we forget that to God, it's all now because He is the Creator of time. Hashem has expectations of us based on our circumstances and provides support where we need it. God modifies the program for each of us, as He has done for all generations throughout time. He is the Provider and Protector of all time.

Now is the perfect time to live with the awareness that we have all we need to live close to God.

Look Low

HOSHANA RABBAH

Hoshana Rabbah literally means "Great Salvation" or "Great Saving." It sounds like the name of a thrift shop. "Hey, kids, let's go to Great Saving to get some deals before Sukkot ends!"

Hoshana Rabbah is the seventh day of Sukkot. It is the last day to eat in the sukkah with a blessing. It is the last day to wave the four species (lulav, etrog, *hadassim*, and *aravot*) with a blessing. *Hoshanot* are prayers said during morning services throughout Sukkot while holding the four species and circling a person holding the Torah on the bimah in synagogue, just as Jews would circle the Altar in the Beit Hamikdash. On Hoshana Rabbah, the congregation circles seven times, as the Jewish People did around the walls of Jericho before entering the Land of Israel to conquer it and settle there.

Hoshana Rabbah is also known as the "Day of the Aravah." It is the day of the custom to "*klap hoshanos*." This is literally hitting the ground with *aravot*, the willow bundle, until the leaves are battered and separate from the branch.

As well as "willow branch," *aravah* can also mean "wilderness." However, according to the Talmud, *Aravah* is the name of the highest of the seven heavens.[1] It is the "place" where God keeps pure *neshamot* (souls). I don't know what that means, but I envision some experience of highest unity with Hashem.

I find meaning in the idea that *Aravah* is the highest heaven and the way these *aravah* branches meet their demise. They are beaten to a pulp, until the leaves lie crushed on the ground. This brings to mind a quote by Carl Jung: "The reason that modern people can't see God is because they won't look low enough."

In our lives, it is often in rock-bottom places, where so much is broken and messy, that we find the best deals.

---

1   *Chagigah* 12b.

Wishful Asking

SHEMINI ATZERET

Ask a clever child what he would wish for if he were granted one wish. He might say, "I'd wish that I could have a wish whenever I wish." This response gets him out of having to identify one desire exclusively.

We have arrived at Shemini Atzeret, the end of the Tishrei marathon. What is the theme of the day? When we know the theme of a festival, we can tap into it with our deeds and requests. On this day, Hashem holds onto us without any particular commandments—only to show His love for us. What should I request on Shemini Atzeret, this day of Hashem's love for the Jewish People? This would seem to be a particularly auspicious time to ask Hashem to fulfill an immediately pressing need.

The *Netivot Shalom* (Rav Sholom Noach Berezovsky, the Slonimer Rebbe, 1911–2000) tells us that on Shemini Atzeret, one should ask that one always be allowed access to the King to speak to Him.

At first, this sounds to me like the clever child's response—like a way out of taking the time to identify a priority. And isn't Hashem always available? Doesn't He continuously grant us access to Him? In my ignorance, I am disappointed by the Slonimer Rebbe's statement. Until I see that Rabbi Moshe Lieber connects this idea to King David's request: "*Achat sha'alti mei'eit Hashem otah avakeish: shivti b'veit Hashem kol yemei chayai*—One thing I ask from Hashem, that I shall request: that I may dwell in the house of Hashem all the days of my life."[1]

King David wanted access to Hashem's presence, to live with Hashem. And something strikes me: Why are there extra words in this request? It seems sufficient to say, "One thing I ask from Hashem, that I may dwell in the house of Hashem all the days of my life." "That I shall request" seems superfluous.

Unless...I wonder if King David was not just asking to be allowed to dwell with Hashem. Perhaps he was asking to have the opportunity to make such a request. Maybe the punctuation could be, "One thing I ask from Hashem: that I shall request that I'll dwell in the house of Hashem." In other words: Please let me request this! My wish is not just to be with You, but to make the request to be with You! In being granted the opportunity to make this request, I am being given the gift of a dynamic relationship with Hashem. Let me remember to speak to Hashem directly and regularly.

When my car won't start in the morning, let me not speak to the car ("C'mon...c'mon!"). Let me entreat the Creator of those who built the car. And when the electricity bill arrives, let me not speak to the envelope ("Seriously? We need to pay again, already?"). Let me speak to the One who created electricity and led people to its discovery. And when my laptop connects quickly to the Internet, let me not just give an undirected sigh of appreciation. Let me direct that sense to the Source of all connections.

Now I have a level of understanding of the idea of the *Netivot Shalom*. While Hashem lovingly holds us for one last day, we remind ourselves of the value of being in a relationship with Him. By requesting that Hashem grant us constant access to him, we are not supposing that He doesn't. We are recognizing that we don't always wish to and remember

---

1   *Tehillim* 27:4.

to speak to Him. On Shemini Atzeret, we ask Hashem to allow our hearts and minds to wish to access Him.

And like that clever child, we want to be able to wish this wish whenever we wish.

Stay

SHEMINI ATZERET

I often feel sad when we come to the end of a festival; I am hesitant to let go. This is why I feel comfort in Shemini Atzeret.

Before the schedule of Torah reading was put into practice (in the time of the Second Beit Hamikdash), culminating in Simchat Torah, that day was just Shemini Atzeret.[1] There is no particular mitzvah to observe on that day. No mitzvah of sukkah or lulav and etrog anymore. Just to be content: "*ach samei'ach.*"

Many commentators mention the concept of Hashem wanting to hold His children close for one more day. "*Kasheh alai preidatchem*" is the wording the Talmud uses to explain God's reasoning for this seemingly extra day. Translated as, "It is hard for Me, your separation," we understand that Hashem does not want to let us go just yet. We have been enjoying an intense closeness from Elul through Rosh Hashanah, Yom Kippur, and culminating in the "time of our joy," Sukkot. Hashem wants to hold on to us this way just a little bit longer.

---

1   *Bamidbar* 29:35.

This idea has long been my comfort—that Hashem doesn't want to let go so fast. Then, a few years ago, I heard a beautiful insight into "*Kasheh alai preidatchem.*" Rabbi Shmuel Silber from Baltimore shared this: The verse can be understood as Hashem saying, "I don't want to let you go yet because once the festival is over, not only will you separate from Me, but *kasheh alai*—it's hard on Me, *preidatchem*—your separation from each other!

Hashem cannot bear to have His children separate from one another. Yamim Tovim are unifying, especially Sukkot, with its lessons regarding the four species, and the unification of all types of Jews. When Yom Tov ends, will we go back to allowing our differences to divide us?

It is "hard" for God when we are separate. Yes, there are many paths within Torah that all lead to Hashem. I may be striving to follow a different valid *mesorah* than the one you follow. This does not have to make me see myself as separate from you. We can both be integral links in the chain of "seventy faces of Torah." And some people may not be following any of the lines of tradition. Still, Hashem wants me to love them, and to see them as among His beloved.

Shemini is "eighth," as in the eighth day of the festival from the beginning of Sukkot. Eight is mystically a number above nature. We need to reach beyond our nature to feel connected to others. Although at our core we are one, this world keeps us separate from our essence and therefore from each other.

Atzeret has four meanings: "refrain [from work]," "gather together," "press out the essence," and "retain." By holding onto us an extra day, we are invited to refrain from falling back into seeing ourselves as separate from others. We are reminded to be together. We are asked to focus on what is real and important—our essence. The final meaning of *atzeret*, retain, can be Hashem telling us that while He is holding onto us with love, He wants us to retain unity throughout the year. We are challenged to grasp the concept of Hashem's "difficulty" in our separateness, and create the space for unity in our hearts.

If not for ourselves, then for Him. And what else is there?

Ready or Not

SIMCHAT TORAH

When was the last time you danced? Dance now, and you can answer, "Now."

Simchat Torah. We are supposed to dance with joy at the idea of having finished the year's cycle of weekly Torah *parashah* readings and immediately beginning again. Are we ready to dance with joy at this prospect?

Some people might say that Jewish ritual is full of "ready or not." A dear friend of mine who was not always Jewish once commented, "Jewish law doesn't care how you feel!" At the time, she was referring to the fact that she had a halachic obligation to eat a certain amount of matzah in the prescribed amount of time, and she was not feeling the least bit hungry.

She was right...and wrong. Jewish law is about preserving our faith while presenting opportunities for us to individually connect with the Source of everything. We are told to eat when we may not feel hungry, to say thank you when we may not feel grateful...to dance when we may not feel joy. (Even to love God when we're not sure what love and God may be...) We know that if we all made our decisions according to our fleeting feelings, we would not be able to be productive members of society, let alone progenitors of the Jewish nation. So my friend was right. Right?

Well, here's the thing. If the sole purpose of Jewish law is to ensure that the Jewish People live, then my friend is correct in her observation: Who cares what you feel? Just do the ritual so that this generation is another link in the chain of Jewish action. But the agenda of halachah is much broader than that. While it is certainly concerned with Jewish continuity, it is primarily an invitation to closeness with God. If we ignore our feelings regarding mitzvah observance, we miss opportunities to better understand ourselves and relate to Hashem with our whole selves. Better to say, "I'm so not hungry, but I am eating this because I want to carry on Judaism and I value my relationship with You," than to not pay attention to how I feel. The latter would be leaving some of myself out of the experience.

We are enjoined to dance on Simchat Torah, to lift our feet and hold each other's hands to the tunes and sounds of our unadulterated singing voices. The expression of our celebration on this day will emanate from our inner collection of *simchah*. How much happiness do we hold? Is there enough for us to dance with a feeling of true joy? Are we ready?

> The expression of our celebration on this day will emanate from our inner collection of *simchah*. How much happiness do we hold?

Well, it's not a surprise party; we knew it was coming. We have had time to prepare, to arouse feelings of gratitude in ourselves leading up to this day, and to bring ourselves to the space of feeling happy to have the Torah as our guide to life. That same friend (who articulated the fact that halachah doesn't care about feelings) cried tears of happiness as we danced together last Simchat Torah to the tune of *"Ashreichem Yisrael*—Fortunate is Israel." Then she marveled, "I know what it's like to live without Torah. I am so happy to have Torah!"

My friend was ready for that dance.

Are we?

Who's Modern Now?

CHANUKAH

The year is 167 BCE. A man stands and calls out, "Whoever is for God, follow me." His name is Mattityahu.

Background: The Syrian Greeks rule over Israel and the surrounding areas. They want modern Greek culture to prevail. Jews following Torah must die because Torah cramps Greek lifestyle, which, aside from philosophical debates, includes worshipping the body, practicing adultery, pedophilia, and infanticide.

Mattityahu has choices: Stand for God and the Jewish nation, or uphold modern Greek culture. The latter is especially inviting, as a Torah lifestyle seems to be outdated. Mattityahu chooses to stand for God, without knowing what the results will be. The efforts are ours, the results, God's.

Roughly 2,200 years later, the results are in! We are the results of that stand. Because of Mattityahu and every Jew who chose Torah before and after him, the Jewish People are here today in the modern world. Think about it: The way Hashem's promise of our survival has played itself out has been through choices of individuals to stand for more than themselves.

The path of Jewish survival follows those who have chosen the eternal relevance of Torah. The descendants of those who chose "modern" Greek culture over Torah are indistinguishable in the world population today, unless those descendants have "turned back" and chosen Torah.

Torah is eternally modern.

Let's get with it!

The path of Jewish survival follows those who have chosen the eternal relevance of Torah.

Thirty-Six

CHANUKAH

With appreciation to Rabbi Pinchas Winston
and his book The Wonderful World of Thirty-Six.

Driving back from New York to Boston one Sunday, I happened upon a Christian radio station urging people to bring their broken selves to the church. The announcer promised, "All you need to do is show up, and God will make you whole."

Hmm, I thought. *That sounds like a great deal. I don't actually have to commit to anything or change my behavior. I don't have to take any responsibility for my actions. I can just sit back and let God do the work...*

If the Maccabees had taken this route, we wouldn't have an excuse to eat oily food every December.

According to Jewish tradition, our job is to not sit back. We are partners with God, giving Him reason to keep us around. When the Maccabees were searching for the pure olive oil, they were not just looking for pure olive oil. They sought something the entire world had lost yet desperately needed. It had made intermittent, disguised

appearances over the years, and now the world needed to have it—
to see it with clarity.

If I find something, I am obligated to put forth efforts to return it
to its owner, according to the Torah. This is the mitzvah of *hashavat
aveidah* (returning lost property).

There is a caveat: If the owner has given up all hope of ever finding
the item, I am absolved of my responsibility to return it. The only One
who could "return" the lost item that the Chashmona'im (Maccabees)
sought was God himself. First, though, someone had to show that hope
was not lost.

Flashback: Creation of the world:

- Day One: God created light and dark.
- Day Four: God created sun, moon, and stars.

So what was the light of the first day? The Talmud teaches that this
was a "spiritual light" that shone for thirty-six hours and was then set
aside for the righteous in the future. It was hidden so that its power
would not be abused by the evil minded. The light was not destroyed. It
was "hidden." Lost to us.

So where is that light? Mystical sources say "In the thirty-six lights of
Chanukah." Thirty-six? Count one the first night, two the second night,
three the third, through the eighth, and add up the numbers: thirty-six.

Flashback continues:

- Adam and Chavah are created.
- They sin and hide.
- God asks Adam, "*Ayekah*—Where are you?"

God didn't know where Man was hiding? The numerical value for the
word *ayekah* is thirty-six.

Years later, Yaakov meets Rachel and wants to marry her.

- God arranges for Leah to marry Yaakov first.
- Leah's name equals thirty-six.
- Rachel is thirty-six years old when she dies.
- Yaakov returns to his parents' home after being away for...
  thirty-six years!

The event leading up to Yaakov's struggle with Eisav's heavenly counterpart seems strange. Yaakov crosses his family over the river and then goes back to collect "small jars." The midrash connects the jars to Chanukah: "Because you troubled yourself for small jars, I will repay your children with a small jar for the Chashmona'im." After Yaakov's struggle, the Torah reads: "And it shone for him, the sun." The word "for him" is *lo—lamed vav*—thirty-six.

When Yaakov died, Yosef put a crown on the coffin. Then the kings of the world placed their crowns around Yosef's. The Gemara in *Sotah* tells us how many crowns there were in all: thirty-six.

Two generations later, when Moshe was born, there was *ohr* (light) in the house. The word *ohr* is in the Torah how many times? Thirty-six!

Moshe was born thirty-six years after the beginning of the actual slavery in Egypt. He is known to have taught the whole Torah to the Jewish People for thirty-six days.[1] There are thirty-six tractates in Talmud, which the midrash says lead to "merit of the great light."

The number thirty-six hints to connecting to that great original light—remember, the one from the first day of creation. When God asks Adam, "*Ayekah*," He wants man to gauge the distance between himself and the light.

Back to the Maccabees. When the battle was won and the priestly family had cleaned up the Beit Hamikdash, they felt the desperate loss of that light. They yearned to bask in the clarity of its glow, to be enveloped in its warmth and its splendor. They were challenging Hashem from the depths of their desire to return the original light to the world, if only for a short while.

It was not just about oil. It was about thirty-six. The fact that Chanukah was established for all time means there is power in this time for us to tap into that original light. The number thirty-six lives in the lights of Chanukah, in the expression of those eight days and nights.

Do we still hold the hope of reclaiming what was lost? Chanukah is the time to look into the thirty-six flames and renew our commitment

---

1   *Seder Olam Rabbah* 10.

to being active in our search, to be willing to do the work necessary to learn and grow, to prove to God that we have not given up hope of finding our way to Him.

Then, He will have no choice but to return to us that lost light, and we will have no choice but to return our lost selves to Him.

Guns and Water

CHANUKAH

There's a gun under my kitchen table. Plus, it's raining outside.

The potato gun is what's left from the children's active inside playtime. It was the weapon of choice for the kids pretending to be the Greeks in this particular game. I see no sign of weaponry left from the Maccabees. I wonder what ammunition they used.

In the Torah reading for Shabbat Chanukah, Pharaoh dreams about cows and wheat. People dream all the time. What so disturbs Pharaoh about his dreams that he desperately seeks satisfying interpretations?

It is no coincidence that we read about Pharaoh's dreams at this time. The small band of priests, the Chashmonai family, also known as Maccabees, fought with all they had. They threw their whole selves into proving that they had not lost their passion for serving God. They knew that the reason Hashem had allowed the Beit Hamikdash to be sullied was because they had not displayed sufficient desire in their service. Their service had become rote.

On Chanukah, we celebrate the victory of the small Jewish resistance defeating the massive, powerful Syrian-Greek army. About sixty generations earlier, when Pharaoh dreamed of skinny cows swallowing fat cows, the vision of this impossibility as reality unsettled him. Yosef, on the other hand, kept Hashem in the picture, so the fact that laws of nature could be suspended was part of his reality. He interpreted the dreams practically for Pharaoh because that was all Pharaoh needed. Yosef carried the balance of living with practicality while knowing that reality is beyond practicality.

Fast-forward to our Chanukah story. When Mattityahu and his family formed their revolt, practicality called for swords and shields. They knew they had to function within the laws of nature. Yet it was their understanding of God's reality that invited their victory. They had no problem believing that skinny cows—a small band of priests—could completely consume fat cows—a massive Greek army. Laws of nature hold, as rainfall nourishes the world. At the same time, the Creator and Sustainer of those laws will change the course at His will.

The potato gun lies forlornly next to some scraps of leftover breakfast. The rain has subsided, and the children are venturing outdoors for a change in adventure. And I make peace with the missing artillery of the Jewish warriors. The properly aimed hearts and minds of the Chashmona'im were their real weapons, and so are ours.

Some things never change.

I'll sweep up under the table now.

Supply and Acceptance of Love

ASARAH B'TEVET

A secret to anticipating each event and then enjoying each moment is letting go of fear and knowing that each circumstance includes opportunities to accept love. Tevet is the month in which Roman troops surrounded the walls of Jerusalem in 69 CE.

It was the beginning of the end.

Our Sages say that the reason the Second Beit Hamikdash was destroyed was because of *sinat chinam*, "baseless hatred" between Jews. I have often wondered what this means. Certainly, people had reasons for disliking one another.

What does *chinam* mean? *Chinam* means "for free." No charge. I'll hate you, free of charge. I want nothing in return, just let me hate you. If someone was offering that, I'd say, "No thanks." There is a lesson in this. If we don't "buy" *sinat chinam*, it can't be sold. If people stop taking the "free" hatred, the supply will be greater than the demand, and then the "hate suppliers" will be forced to abandon this product. Sometimes, we accept hatred because we think we deserve it. We block ourselves from receiving love because we don't think we deserve it. We assume we need to be perfect to be loved. As long as we find a twisted comfort in accepting free hatred, the supply will flow.

Before the Second Beit Hamikdash was destroyed, great Torah scholars exchanged profound understandings and practiced the ritual laws. Yet too many of them missed the boat. They lost focus and forgot that Hashem resided in them. Had more of the Jews been conscious of Hashem's presence, they would not have accepted any free hatred, and the supply of *sinah* (hatred) would have dwindled. Yet too many Jews forgot that they were Godly, and the seeds of hatred grew in those forgetting minds.

The Beit Hamikdash is still not rebuilt. This means that free hatred still festers among us. We're still "buying" the hatred. We need to grow the demand for *ahavat chinam*: love, free of charge.

We need to know we are deserving of love simply because we have souls. When we accept, free of charge, offers of love, the supply of *ahavah* will increase. And the seeds of love will grow in these remembering minds.

Where Faith and Patience Grow

TU B'SHEVAT

When I was seven, my father left me.

In a gas station.

By mistake.

And I was fine.

I had gone to use the public restroom, and when I exited, our car was gone. I found a gas station man and told him that my dad would come back to get me. I knew this with absolute certainty. Sure enough, ten minutes later, that station wagon rolled up with my four roughhousing brothers in the back. I vaguely recall my Abba apologizing profusely to me, with a tinge of incredulity—as if he could not understand how he could possibly have done such a thing! Then, I climbed into the car, and we headed home.

Donald Winnicott, pediatric psychoanalyst, wrote about the "good enough" mother. "The 'good enough' mother often, but not always, responds to her child," he writes. With this mother, the child learns that basic needs will be met, yet there is space for faith and patience to grow. In a sense, the "perfect" mother would only harm her child—by training him to expect immediate responses to his desires, the child would grow unrealistic expectations of the world and relationships.

Also, by not allowing him to experience any prolonged sense of wanting, he would not come to appreciate that which does come to him. He would grow to expect everything and appreciate nothing. There would be no ceiling on his desires, and the idea of restrictions would feel threatening to his very existence. It is the fallibility of the parent that allows faith and patience to grow in the child. In understanding the limitations of mankind, it reminds the child that he and others are not God.

Ironically, it is accepting imperfection that opens to us the ways in which we can be Godlike. For God knows we are limited—and He loves us, forgives us, and remains faithful to us. As we say in *Modeh Ani* every morning, "Who has returned my soul to me with compassion. Great is Your faithfulness." Hashem gives me a new day because He believes in me. Not because I am perfect, but because I am "good enough" to make something of my day.

Tu B'Shevat is the new year for the trees regarding yearly *maaser* (tithing) and counting to the *shemittah* (sabbatical year for the land in Israel). By the fifteenth of Shevat in the Land of Israel, the soil is saturated enough that trees planted after Tu B'Shevat will take root. The *B'nei Yissaschar*, an eighteenth-century commentator, tells us that this is the optimum time to pray for a beautiful etrog. But Sukkot is eight months away! I'm supposed to be thinking about this particular one of the four species now?

This idea is not just about the tangible citron that we'll shake with the lulav on Sukkot. The etrog represents the ideal Jew: It has both a taste and smell, and this duality represents a person who has both good deeds and Torah learning—the person we ideally want to be.

And what better time to ask for help in becoming our ideal selves than when winter weighs heavily on us, and we can feel limited. So before we even see signs of growth, we display faith that Hashem will help us blossom, and we will have to exhibit patience throughout the process. Not the kind of patience that has us pacing and checking our phones every ten seconds. Rather, the kind that has us accepting that which we cannot change as we await the arrival of what's to come.

When my father accidentally left me, he was being "good enough." Although he would have preferred not to have lost track of his only daughter, his human error allowed me to grow my faith: I got to experience what it means to know with absolute certainty that my father would not abandon me, and to wait patiently for what comes next.

Which, in my case, because this was also pre-seatbelt laws, was a roughhousing ride home.

Through Candy
and Ulterior Motives

PURIM

An actual conversation:

Our six-year-old daughter: "Imma, when someone dies, can I eat a doughnut?"

Me: "What?"

Six: "Can I eat a doughnut when someone dies?"

Me: "Why are you asking this question?"

Six: "Because my *morah* (teacher) said when a person dies, we eat round things."

Me: "What round things did she say we eat?"

Six: "Eggs. But I like doughnuts."

Me: "Well, when someone dies, we feel sad because we miss them, so that's not the best time for a doughnut."

Six: "But we could all go together to a kosher Dunkin Donuts and buy a whole box."

Me: "At another time, maybe, but not right when someone dies."

Six: "Okay, so when?"

I seriously could not make this stuff up.

Kids want yummy-tasting stuff. Always. One comedian comments that the entire theme of his childhood could be summed up in two words: Get Candy. People can run their entire lives on this idea. More sophisticated items take the place of lollipops, but it's all just glorified candy.

When a child in a Jewish day school begins to learn Torah, the teacher makes a *Chumash* party. The children receive their new *Chumashim* amid much fanfare and cake. What's the point of that party? Don't we want our children to learn Torah for its own sake? Shouldn't the child know that the reason for Torah study is to touch Godliness? Why are we throwing in the icing?

Children do not understand the sweetness of the words, ideas, and instructions they are about to learn. They understand that cake tastes pleasant. The teacher and parents hope that Torah learning will be associated with pleasure so that the child will be driven to keep learning. The Talmud tells us, *"Mi'toch she'lo lishmah, ba lishmah."*[1] Loosely translated, this means, "From non-altruistic reasons come altruistic reasons."

Meaning, from doing something right for the wrong reasons, we'll (eventually) come to do that action for the right reasons. This is the rationale behind going through the motions of ritual, even when our hearts aren't in it. A friend of my husband pointed out that the interesting grammar of the first word is the key to understanding the phrase: *mi'toch* literally means "from through," which makes the meaning "from going through the non-altruism we come to altruism."

If we hope to ever reach greater levels of intention in our actions, we must go through the ulterior motives. We must recognize that the child always has ulterior motives, and that does not make him or her wrong. It simply makes him or her a child. If we pretend that ulterior motives

---

1   *Pesachim* 50b.

don't exist or we think they make us bad, we miss the opportunity to move through them.

Furthermore, this understanding brings us not only to stop avoiding our non-altruistic motivations; it actually invites us to seek those motivations in order to travel through them to reach a place of less ulterior motives. In other words, the *"lo lishmah"* is the path to the *"lishmah"*!

> If we hope to ever reach greater levels of intention in our actions, we must go through the ulterior motives.

In one horrible memory, one of our older sons recalls being at his *Chumash* play, the official kick-off of Torah study in school. The children were five and six years old, and the cake was being handed out by a poor educator (yes, they exist). The child next to our son was reaching for the biggest piece of cake on the platter, when the bad educator swatted the child's hand, saying, "You're being greedy. Now you don't get a piece."

I am sick when I recall this story, as is our son. Thank God, our son grew to realize who was wrong in the scenario. That "educator" ruined a perfectly good path through *lo lishmah*. He could have pointed out with good humor and a wink that the child's desire for the big piece shows how big his enjoyment of Torah learning can be.

Purim involves physical celebration. We celebrate our physical existence, which Amalek/Haman wanted to do away with. We eat and drink and make merry, like King Achashveirosh did. Only not, because Achashveirosh's festivities were an end, while our festivities are a means. A means to show ourselves and the King that our existence matters to us and that we appreciate and desire life for the opportunities it presents. If we think parties are the purpose of living, we will celebrate like Achashveirosh, partying hard while thinking, *What else is there?*

When we grow to know why we celebrate, we can be grown-up enough to enjoy our very existence for what it is: an opportunity to be close to Hashem through our daily actions. Then life can be a party—with or without doughnuts.

Being Yaakov's Children

PURIM

My parents were serving as a rabbinical couple in Claremont synagogue in Cape Town, South Africa, when there was a terrorist attack in Israel. Two of the casualties in Israel were grandchildren of Claremont members, and many synagogue members were adamant that Purim festivities be suspended in light of the tragedy.

My father called a *rav* in Israel to seek advice. The *rav* said, "I will tell you what my personal response is, and why I am celebrating Purim vibrantly with my community and our children. These evil people have taken so much from us. I'm not going to let them also take away our Purim!"

Needless to say, Claremont celebrated rousingly, with heightened awareness of the importance of coming together for *smachot* (joyous occasions). And those who celebrated rose above nature.

Rabbi Abie Rotenberg composed a soul-stirring song entitled "The Man from Vilna." It tells of an elderly man traveling to a family *simchah*.

The man explains that "no *simchah* is a burden." He is a Holocaust survivor, and in the song, he tells a story of his younger self: After the war, he and some other "lost souls" returned to their hometown to search for vestiges of their former lives. What they found was desolation. The streets that had housed vibrant families lay in ruins. The men wandered despairingly through the destruction until one man pointed out that the shul was still standing, and as Simchat Torah was that night, they could dance with the Torah! Leading the way, he ran through the barricades into the desecrated house of prayer. Desperate to hold a *Sefer Torah*, the men flung open the doors of the *aron kodesh* (sacred ark), only to find there was no *Sefer Torah*.

Just when one might think this was too hard a test of faith, some of the men thought to lift up the two children who had been traveling with them. And the chorus goes, "We danced round and round in circles, as if the world had done no wrong, from evening until morning, filling up the shul with song. Though we had no *Sefer Torah* to gather in our arms, in its place we held those children, the Jewish People would live on..." Where a natural response would be hopelessness, those men chose hope.

Our enemies continually seek to destroy us because they are obsessed with controlling that which is outside themselves, with nary a thought of controlling themselves. We need to be different, to introspect and to ask ourselves, "What does Hashem want me to do?"

This is the way we control our internal worlds, our choices, and our responses. This is the way we create *simchah* within ourselves and within any space.

And this is the way we rise above the urge to despair and choose instead to celebrate.

Tough and Humble

PESACH

The Pesach Seder is about my mother, and not just because she makes matzah balls. My mother teaches second grade, and she's tough! She's one of those teachers who is in control of her classroom. You know those teachers? The ones who set ground rules and follow through. The ones whose main focus is to facilitate social and academic growth in each student. The ones not afraid of the students—or the parents.

They are the best. Their classrooms are havens of learning, and that is my mother's classroom. My mother hasn't always taught second grade. For years, she taught kindergarten. Then, when I was twelve, my mother went back to school for her master's degree in computer education, and she taught in the computer room at a high school for kids with behavioral problems. My brothers and I loved to hear about those experiences, especially about the time my mother had to hold a kid down till the police came. That kid never messed with my mother again.

About that tough thing, my brother is fond of saying, "If Ema was a spy and enemies captured her, no matter what they tried, they'd get nothing out of her!" That being said, my mother is the most humble person I know. While she will happily dispense advice about almost anything she knows, my mother is always open to learn more. She is an avid reader of health tips and educational innovations. She loves attending *shiurim* and informative lectures.

When my mother was the rebbetzin of a large congregation in South Africa, she was teaching bat mitzvah girls and adults, and she was a source of wise advice for many. At the same time, she set up a *chavruta* for herself to learn *Chumash* and *Rashi*, which she'd never formally had a chance to learn. I know my mother would wonder why I see this as so admirable. Here's the thing—it's about humility. My mother had no problem with the idea of breaking her teeth over a *Rashi* while she held a prominent position in the community. That takes three things:

- An understanding that opportunities for growth are ever available
- A prioritization of that growth
- A recognition that the only opinion that really counts is Hashem's

These contain the essence of humility, and that's what defines my mother.

At the Seder, we remind ourselves that as tough as we are, and as much as we've endured, there's more to learn. Seder night is set up to engage the children, because we are meant to each engage the child in ourselves who knows there are so many questions to be asked and so much to learn. This night is the opportunity to free ourselves from the arrogance that holds us back from seeking growth.

My mother, throughout the year, understands that lesson well: with the exception of drinking four glasses of wine, munching on *maror*, and a few other activities, my mother basically lives every day like it's Seder night.

Jump. Start.

PESACH

The title was misleading.

Choose Your Own Adventure. These books were popular for kids in the '80s. You would read a few pages of a story, and then you would get to something like...

- "If you want to go with your friend to the abandoned shipyard, turn to page seventeen."
- "If you want to stay home to work on your science fair project, turn to page twenty-three."

You would turn to the page of your choice and find out what happened next. You might find a treasure in the shipyard and then get to choose whether to keep it or bring it to the police department. You might be swallowed by the frog that turned into a dragon as a result of your science experiment. Then you'd find the dreaded words "The End," in which case, you could just turn back to the beginning and choose a different adventure.

Still, the title was a misnomer:

- You didn't really get to choose your adventure.
- The adventures were already written.
- You got to choose your decision.

When it comes to making a decision, a healthy approach usually involves considering consequences until we feel comfortable enough with a choice that seems the better one. This is when our decisions involve two or more equally important options. Then there are times when the choice is about action or inaction. If such a choice existed in *Choose Your Own Adventure*, it would read: "If you want to continue, turn to page 54. If not, close the book."

These decisions are between "Do it" or "Don't do it."

If the "it" is good, here's where we need the *middah* (character trait) of *zerizut* (swift action). When the Jews left Egypt, they did so quickly. The Torah tells us that they left so fast, the dough they carried did not have time to rise. This has given rise to the idea that it took less than eighteen minutes for the following amount of people to leave Egypt: six hundred thousand men between the ages of twenty and sixty, plus all the women, plus all the older men, plus all the children, plus all their cattle and stuff.

The Exodus was not a time for patience, it was not a time for contemplation, and it was not a time to hold on or hold back. It was a time to let go and move forward. Haste mattered.

Did you ever ride a professional zip line? You stand at the top of the wall, thirty feet or so above ground. You look down. (Or not.) You are attached to the harness. You know with your intellect that you are safe, yet a very loud voice of what seems to be reason, yells, "NO! Don't do it!" To experience the adventure, you need to decide to *not* listen to that voice. The thing is, when you decide to *not* do something, you think about that something until you *do* something else. So in the instant you decide to not listen to that voice, you need to stop thinking and just jump!

This is *zerizut*. It is the answer to the voice of inaction. *Zerizut* says, "This is not a discussion. Your suggestion does not warrant attention."

Zerizut is like the parent getting into the driver's seat, starting the engine, and driving, while her three-year-old is shouting, "No I don't want to go. I want to stay home!" *Zerizut*'s action is the response that says, "Regardless of the considerations to remain right where we are, we're going!"

The voice of inaction can be deafening (I WANT TO STAY HOME!). When heeding that voice is preventing us from doing what needs to be done, we must know that we have the power to deem that voice irrelevant.

When I was a kid, my parents had an abbreviation they would throw between each other whenever we children were being ridiculous. "IIB"—Ignore Irrelevant Behavior. While psychoanalysts will confirm that no behavior is innately irrelevant, what my parents were doing was purposely not reinforcing undesirable behavior. By paying no mind to whining and passing moods, they were not feeding into unhelpful speech and behaviors. In that way, we had to find more mature ways to get attention or be heard.

The voice in our minds that urges us not to take action is like the voices of the kids in the back of the car. We can decide not to listen, not to make a big deal about it. To deem it irrelevant. To keep going about our business of action. When the Jews were leaving Egypt, they had to go quickly before the voices of "Don't do it" might have overpowered them.

When it comes to *zerizut*, the zip line can represent any opportunity that arises throughout the day: caring for a family member, attending that support group, or simply smiling at your spouse. It's about seizing the opportunity of the moment before it passes, and it's about letting go of the "Don't do it" before it stops us from doing the right thing.

Lady J., beloved wife of Lord Jakobovits, former Chief Rabbi of the United Kingdom, was known to say, "Thank before you think." She would express streaming appreciation throughout her adult life. Saying thank you was a decision-turned-commitment-turned-habit, born of the idea that if you start to think about it, you may find reason not to do it: "What if she'll feel I want something from her?" "What if he thinks I'm being 'holier than thou?'" Reasons not to say thank you? Lady J. let them go, and seized each moment.

If we resolve not to listen to that voice as it recurrently protests our movement, and we stick to that decision enough times, something happens: the voice changes. As we stand atop that zip line wall, poised to jump again, the voice mumbles something like, "Oh, never mind, you're not listening anyway...you never do. Just jump already. Get it over with." Then the new challenge is to consciously infuse each jump/ good deed with feeling so that it carries meaning.

As we move toward Pesach, we hope to be free of what holds us back from our best selves. While we don't really choose our own adventures, we get to choose decisions. When faced with the option to do good or not, we can employ "IIB" for the voice that says, "Don't do it." We can act *b'zerizut*. We can jump from the zip line wall, the proverbial fence of indecision. We can turn the page instead of closing the book. And then, until The End, the adventure continues.

Happy (about Your) Birthday!

PESACH

Chavivah, four, has a plan: Decorate the house and shout, "Happy Birthday!" when Abba comes home.

"But it's not Abba's birthday," I say.

She says, "It doesn't matter."

I think about that—how we, as Jews, celebrate being Jewish more often than just on our birthday.

Our birthday is Pesach. Six hundred thousand Jewish men between the ages of twenty and sixty, and all the women, children, and older men who left the place of death, marched toward their destiny on the fifteenth of the Jewish month of Nissan, just over 3,300 years ago.

While we formally celebrate our national birthday yearly, we make mention of the Exodus every single day in our structured prayers and blessings. In a sense, we get to celebrate our existence daily.

There is a depth of truth in Chavivah's innocent statement: "It doesn't matter." It's not the anniversary of the day you were born? So what! I will celebrate your birthday today simply because I'm happy you were born.

So I tell the four-year-old that we can decorate and celebrate. Her eyes light up.

I know it's just because she thinks she's getting cake. Still...it doesn't matter.

Let the Liberation Continue

SEFIRAT HAOMER

Seder night.

We have lots of food throwing and wild rapping, among other untraditional activities to keep the little (and big) ones interested and awake. Between the crazy stuff and the text of the Haggadah, we try to remind each other to recognize our personal "Egypts," and feel hopeful that God will help us to be free from bondage in our lives, because we know He wants only what's best for us.

There's usually more than one thing holding us back from being more.

Here's one: How difficult it is to be around people who want you to take responsibility for their feelings. It can feel stifling if you let them. You can be enslaved to their desire for you to make them happy.

In his book *Nonviolent Communication*, Marshall Rosenberg writes about the stages from emotional slavery to emotional liberation.

1. In the first stage, we are enslaved. Every relationship feels like a burden, as we carry the idea that we need to make everyone happy. We do not recognize, value, or communicate our own needs clearly. Any giving in this stage is out of fear, guilt, or the desire to relieve ourselves of the urgent, overwhelming heaviness of another's unhappiness that we think we need to fix.

2. In the second stage, we cast off the burden of that "responsibility," sometimes angrily (with a sense that we've been taken advantage of). We then become enslaved to our own needs and feelings. We hold a "that's your problem!" attitude regarding others and become unkind when relating to their feelings. We disregard the value of caring for another.

(Both stages 1 and 2 sound like teenagers to me, and like adults who never outgrew their adolescence...and sometimes that's most of us when we're tired and stretched.)

3. Stage three, emotional liberation, comes when we have learned to take responsibility for clearly expressing our needs in a way that shows respect and concern for others. Our giving at this stage comes from a choice to be compassionate. We are free to care for ourselves and others thoughtfully, genuinely, joyfully.

We are moving through the forty-nine days of counting from Pesach until Shavuot, when we received the Torah at Har Sinai. The Torah was offered to people who had just been set free from a life that had made it nearly impossible to make choices that bound them to Hashem. This was because they had been living under constant threat of drastic repercussions for shirking mandated expectations from a master who cared not at all for their well-being. To my mind, that idea makes the Omer time a perfect space to assess and work on our emotional freedom.

During these forty-nine days, I can decide whose thoughts, feelings, and opinions should matter enough to me to impact my decisions. I can work to move away from serving people whose "mandated" expectations keep me from making healthy, thoughtful choices. I can move toward emotional liberation. Then I'll be striving to receive Torah and do the will of the One Who wants only what's best for me.

Arriving at Compassion

SEFIRAT HAOMER

We are counting the days and weeks from Pesach until Shavuot; from physical freedom to the acceptance of that which will free us to reach our ultimate potential. We count seven weeks. Each week, we work on perfecting a different character trait.

- The first week is *chessed*, which is "kindness."
- The second week is *gevurah*, which is "discipline."
- The third week is *tiferet*, which can be translated as "beauty" or "compassion."

In English, the word "beauty" represents a vague idea. As *tiferet* balances the first two traits, defining it as "compassion" suits our understanding for now. The first two traits, kindness and discipline, seem straightforward enough, and now we need to add compassion to the mix. What is the difference between kindness and compassion?

- Kindness is an act. Compassion is a feeling.
- Kindness is giving a sandwich to a hungry child. Compassion is feeling some of that child's desperation.

Kindness, *chessed*, is a foundational trait—we must learn to give. Yet if we give only at the *chessed* level, we hold ourselves back from growing. *Tiferet* is a higher level in the spiritual spheres. Reaching for *tiferet* means reaching beyond the mannerisms of giving. And we are only truly living with *tiferet* when we live continually with the balance of *chessed* and *gevurah*—kindness and discipline.

Two facts we need to know in order to grow *tiferet*:

1. Compassion is a developed emotion.
2. Compassion requires imagination.

Regarding fact 1, many of us unfortunately carry the myth that our feelings are just "there," and that there is nothing to do about feelings but act on them, let them be, or deny them. We may not know that we have the power to develop feelings, and Hashem wants us to develop our feelings in our service of Him.

Regarding fact 2, adults are prone to relegating imagination to the archives of long-lost childhood playtime. Remember when we imagined ourselves in situations we had never experienced? We could feel the triumph of slaying a dragon, or the terror of being locked up in a dungeon by an evil witch! The feelings were real.

> Even if I have never experienced your loss, I can imagine your pain.

We still have the power of imagination. In being compassionate, I arouse in myself a sense of sharing your burden. Even if I have never experienced your loss, I can imagine your pain.

Let's (re)discover our capacity to develop depth of feelings for each other.

Let's (re)discover the gifts of our imaginations.

And let's experience the beauty of *tiferet*.

Angels Don't Eat!

SHAVUOT

I enjoy a good read, specifically realistic fiction and anything based on a true story.

To me, modern cookbooks fall under that category. You know those ones with magnificent photographs of perfectly presented cuisine on exquisite fine china in newly renovated kitchens or on flawlessly decorated dining room tables that no child has come within ten feet of? Those books are real page-turners. (I must see which recipes I'll never precisely follow.) And suspenseful. (What would happen if I actually bought all the proper ingredients and used measuring spoons? We'll never know.)

When I read those cookbooks, I also get curious: Why spend time crushing juniper berries and peppercorns for a "skirt steak" (clearly fodder for Amelia Bedelia), when you can, say, not do that?

On Shavuot, one of the offerings in the Beit Hamikdash was *shtei halechem*, two wheat flour loaves. By contrast, forty-nine days earlier, the *omer* offering, which kick-started the count-up from the Exodus to the receiving of God's Torah, was simple barley flour.

The *omer* offering was brought on Pesach, when we were doing an extreme purge of materialism. We were freeing ourselves from the constraints of physicality. The irony of the *omer* offering was that once we brought that offering, barley products from the new grain crop became permitted to us. So once we displayed our ability to separate ourselves from materialism, God then granted us…materialism.

While this may seem backward, once we understand that the ability to "live without" is not the end goal, it actually makes perfect sense. "Living without" is a prerequisite to properly "living with." If I am completely dependent on creature comforts, I will not grant those comforts the respect they deserve. I will not appreciate those comforts as gifts from Hashem. And I'll be in danger of abusing those comforts—of using them exclusively to satisfy my human desires, without awareness of their intrinsic purpose.

One of the five names of Shavuot is *Chag Hakatzir*, "Festival of the Harvest." Harvesting is gathering ripened crops from the fields. Just before Shavuot, the wheat crop is harvested, and from that gathering, wheat berries are ground into flour, dough is formed, and bread is baked. Two loaves from that first gathering are brought as the commanded "*shtei halechem*." And then the new crop—this time wheat—is permitted to us.

We can easily understand why the *omer* offering is not loaves of bread, as it is offered on Pesach, when we do not eat bread. Yet with a superficial understanding of what chametz represents (i.e., materialism), perhaps the Shavuot offering should also be unleavened? Yet it is not.

The *omer* offering is basic. It is offered at a time when we are detoxing from the physical. We are completely separating from *chametz*, which represents our *yetzer hara*, our ego. Leavened food, on the other hand, contains ingredients unnecessary for basic sustenance. When we live with more than the basics, the extras can easily become obstacles to connection with Hashem. The more "stuff" we own, the more we can be distracted from our true reason for living. So shouldn't the Shavuot offering also be simple? After all, we are receiving the Torah, which, like water and light, is pretty much all we need.

Here's the thing: While we need a good detox once a year, there is a better way to live than separating ourselves from materialism. And there is a process, a journey we need to move through, in order to arrive at this better way. The forty-nine days from Pesach to Shavuot are the perfect days for this process. Shavuot is the time of the giving of the Torah—the time that the purpose for the Exodus from Egypt was realized. Each of the forty-nine days represents a step away from the crushing Egyptian servitude toward service that frees our souls—service to God. We also move away from the simple barley-flour offering of Pesach toward the offering of leavened loaves for Shavuot. With all the work we did before Pesach to purge our homes of leavened items, we might conclude that it is somehow holier to eat unleavened food than leavened food.

In *Parashat Kedoshim*, Hashem commands us to be holy, sanctified.[1] How do I be holy? "Sanctify yourselves with what is permitted to you."[2] In other words, the mitzvah to be holy is not referring to abstaining from that which is forbidden (nonkosher). Being holy is reached by exercising self-control specifically in the areas of pleasures that are permitted to us. The *Shelah* tells us that to be *kadosh*, we need to be particular with our conduct in two specific areas: eating and intimacy. These carry potential for unparalleled closeness to Hashem.

Exercising self-control does not mean complete abstention. It means conscious, disciplined involvement. And enjoyment! When I know how and when to resolutely say "no," or "not now," my "yes" can be wholehearted, and I can feel pleasure in partaking. This is the way Hashem wants us to live throughout the year.

The Torah was given to human beings, much to the initial dismay of the celestial beings, a.k.a. angels. According to *Midrash Rabbah*, Hashem quieted the objections of the angels by showing them Avraham's face and reminding them that they should be ashamed for trying to withhold

---

1   *Vayikra* 19:2.
2   *Yevamos* 20a.

Torah from the one (Avraham) in whose home they had eaten.[3] Such a strange way to quiet them...

- It was Moshe who was the chosen medium for dissemination of Torah. Why does the midrash bring Avraham into the picture?
- What does food have to do with deserving Torah?

As my kids would say when someone follows a question with a question that hints to the answer to the first question: *"Exactly."*

Torah is for those who are involved in worldly living. The Talmud portrays Moshe as the one to hush the angels. Moshe challenged the celestial beings to see if any of the Ten Commandments applied to them. The midrash, though, adds a reminder of the episode with Avraham and his angel guests, as if to say, not only is Torah for those who live in circumstances that allow for mitzvah observance, Torah is for those involved in physical activities that may seem mundane. And angels don't eat.

One year, as the Rabbinical couple at our communal Shavuot meal, my husband and I performed an entertaining presentation for the members of our congregation in Sea Point, Cape Town, South Africa. We presented ourselves as four individuals. We each played two roles. We entered one at a time, disguised as a Jewish character with a particular dilemma:

- I first portrayed an observant single woman who considers lowering her standards of Shabbat and *kashrut* observance in the hopes of broadening her base of eligible partners.
- My second character was a mom bent on forbidding her teenage son from attending yeshiva out of fear that he would "become so kosher," he would no longer eat his mother's homemade food.
- My husband played a man who did not see any benefit in belonging to an Orthodox shul, since he did not consider himself observant.

---

3   *Shemot* 28:1.

- In the last role, my husband acted as an angry Israeli who boldly challenges Jews who dare to call themselves Zionists while living in the Diaspora.

Besides being highly amusing, our presentation had a purpose: to confront people with familiar dilemmas in the hope of finding the inspiration to focus on valuable solutions and attitudes. The activity was interactive. Members were encouraged to suggest ideas or sympathize with or challenge each personality. We *davka* played out this drama on the eve of the day we relive the acceptance of Torah, because we wanted the relationship with Torah to emerge as the most useful guide in our personal decision-making: Regarding Torah, we are told, *"Lo ba'Shamayim hi*—It is not in Heaven."[4]

Torah's application is not restricted to global or obviously spiritual situations. Torah applies to the details of our individual physical lives. Torah's application also extends to what we might call the extras: the leaven or the cherries (or juniper berries) on top. So while I ponder the questionable reality of those glossy cookbook photographs, and I wonder why the author/chef assumes I have any idea what "aioli" is, I can also savor the awareness that it is precisely our involvement in details of all things physical that binds us to Torah—Hashem's eternal gift.

---

4   *Devarim* 30:12.

Unlimited Perspective

SHAVUOT

Before Har Sinai became the famous landmark of God's revelation to the entire Jewish nation, and the place of the giving of the Torah, it was home to a burning bush. There, Moshe questioned God's faith in the merit of the Jewish People. The way Moshe saw it, the Jews were an enslaved, weary nation who had fallen into idolatry and practices far from Hashem's holy realm.

What made them worthy of being redeemed from Egypt? Hashem allayed Moshe's suspicions by explaining that fifty days after the Exodus, the Jews would surround the very place where Moshe now stood and they would receive the Torah, thus justifying all creation and world history. Moshe seems almost disrespectful as he stands in the presence of the Almighty before a miraculously un-consuming fire, doubting God's plan of action:

- Why didn't Moshe just accept Hashem's directive that he be the leader for the redemption of the Jewish People?

- When Moshe wonders why Hashem is telling him to be the leader of the enslaved nation, why didn't Hashem respond, "Because I said so!"?

Perhaps, in questioning his own (and his brethren's) merit, Moshe was requesting something. Perhaps he was not content to just accept and set aside his own concerns; he wanted something more. Maybe, by articulating his human capacity for doubt and skepticism, Moshe was asking Hashem to grant him a slice of God's capacity for clarity and faith. Moshe could have done as he was told, no questions asked. On the surface, this may seem the proper way to fulfill God's will, yet there is another way.

Assuming that Moshe wanted to approach life's challenges with Godliness, it follows that Moshe would protest, not necessarily because he wanted out—but because he wanted in. Man's view is blocked by the facade of separate tenses, while God's view includes the breathtaking vistas of vast spiritual potential in each person, place, and thing, beyond time and space.

Perhaps Moshe wanted to be privy to a view beyond his limited one. Moshe's excuses display the idea that his perspective of himself and the Jews was not enough for him to approach his mission as faithfully as he would have liked to. The perspective Hashem provides for Moshe involves the fact that the Jewish People, including Moshe himself, would become receivers of Torah.

The festival of Shavuot. We received the Torah—our guide to a meaningful and pleasurable life. We can strive to fulfill its laws, no questions asked. Alternatively, we can strive to fulfill it with the awareness that the more Torah we receive and internalize, the more Godly our perspective can be, so the more faithfully we can invest in our missions.

Postscripts

Humor and Reality

I love buying Israeli products. Not just because I get to support the Israeli economy but because I get to laugh.

Ever buy clothing in Israel? There is usually something unnecessary attached. Like an extra pocket in an odd place or one side of a snap on each hip with a lacy material draped down the seam.

Then there are the birthday cards wishing you "Long love and last hippyness." The spelling on packaging makes me wonder if these are the same people who e-mail me from Nigeria asking me to wire money so that I will be rich with them.

Today's humor came courtesy of Galil sunflower seeds: First we get the company's slogan—"Taste something extraodinary" (yes, no *r*). And, as proof that these are no "odinary" seeds, we're informed that these are "roastes" sunflower seeds! Then, because apparently eating *garinim* can be quite mysterious, we are reassured that "the secret is in the taste!" (What!?) Also, to add to the intrigue, there is a picture on the bottom of the label displaying walnuts, pistachios, and hazelnuts—all fine nuts, but not what's in the bag. And, finally, in case we were concerned about the amount of moisture in the product, we discover that eight ounces is the "net wet."

The *Malbim*, a nineteenth-century Russian-born halachic scholar, reminds us that while matter comes into being before its purpose is realized, the vision of the purpose exists first. If we think that the end goal of the material is material, then the packaging can invite frustration:

291

- Is there nobody who will stand against unnecessary designs on clothing?!
- Are there no English-speaking people at the plant?!

I expect certain things to be, and I am affected when reality does not meet my expectations. I can feel annoyed, helpless, or simply amused when the unexpected occurs. Another option is to laugh. The less I feel threatened by a situation, the more easily I will laugh.

When we sing, "*Az yimalei sechok pinu*—Then our mouths will be filled with laughter,"[1] we are referring to a time when God's presence will be clear to all. When we develop a solid sense of self and a firm grounding in faith that the beginning and end is God, we will feel less bothered by the unexpected. We will more readily accept strangeness as part of the package filled with good stuff.

And we will laugh more often.

If at First

Lest we value the end result over the effort involved...

It's early. Sunrise early. Godly hour. I hear a sound. I stealthily get out of bed and peek out my bedroom door. I have a clear view of the living room window and the porch just beyond.

My daughter is out there, on the porch. She's six. Just. She's on the bike she can't ride yet, the bike her older sister was trying to teach her to ride yesterday. I stand back from the window, where she doesn't see me. She attempts to balance and pedal. She harnesses her efforts; she wants to ride that bike. The goal is her motivation. She thinks nobody is watching. I watch, and I am overcome, with...what is it? Affection. Admiration.

I watch my child voluntarily rehearsing undisturbed, untainted by influences outside herself. She desires to master this new skill, and she will try, try again, until she succeeds—and she will succeed. And I'll be proud, no doubt. We'll all be proud, and we'll applaud, and she'll be bursting with a sense of satisfaction. Her exhilaration will come

---

1   *Tehillim* 126:2.

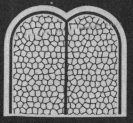

MOSAICA PRESS
BOOK PUBLISHERS

Elegant, Meaningful & Bold

info@MosaicaPress.com
www.MosaicaPress.com

The Mosaica Press team of
acclaimed editors and designers
is attracting some of the most
compelling thinkers and teachers
in the Jewish community today.
Our books are available around
the world.

HARAV YAACOV HABER
RABBI DORON KORNBLUTH

About the Author

D'vorah Miller has been teaching children and adults about Judaism, relationships, self-esteem, and spirituality for over thirty years across four continents. She has edited several books, published articles, and posted videos on effective parenting and personal growth based on Torah teachings. D'vorah served as assistant to the Regional Director and Alumni Coordinator for New England NCSY. D'vorah and her husband, Rabbi Shmuel Miller, served as a rabbinical couple of Ohr Somayach synagogue in Cape Town, South Africa, and she was Director of Jewish Studies at Irvine Hebrew Day School in Orange County, California.

At present, D'vorah designs curriculum, teaches, and mentors educators for Ikaron, an Orange County–based Hebrew school. D'vorah also facilitates learning at the Hebrew Academy of Huntington Beach. She holds a Judaic studies teaching certification from Bnot Chayil College in Jerusalem, Israel; a general teaching certification from New South Wales Board of Education in Sydney, Australia; and a certification in therapeutic counseling from MST College in London, England.

D'vorah and her husband are the blessed parents of eight great kids and at least as many grandkids. D'vorah is available for speaking engagements and educational mentorship. She and her husband together are available for marriage workshops and as scholars in residence for organizational events. She can be reached at dbm613@gmail.com.

when she realizes she can ride freely, without falling, and that will be good. Then.

Yet to me, this is better. Now. I am exhilarated now as she attempts to pedal and she falls and gets up. Again, over and over. I am inspired by that determination. If I have to choose which time I prefer—this effort time or the later success time—I choose this time, hands down. When I see that my child has such a strong desire to master a skill, and she is willing to work hard, privately, and fall hard in order to get there, it's priceless.

I stand a moment longer. My heart swells with pride, and my eyes tear. I offer a silent prayer that she finds the strength to get up each time she falls. Then I tiptoe back to bed.

And my little rider is none the wiser about how she inspires wisdom in me.

The Blessed Defense

V'ZOT HABERACHAH

"And this is the blessing with which Moshe, man of God, blessed the children of Israel before he died."

Why is Moshe described here as *"ish ha'Elokim*—man of God"?

Pesikta D'Rav Kahana, a collection of midrash compiled in the late 1800s, says the term "man of God" is reserved for a person who speaks in defense of the Jewish People. Rav Avraham Saba, a late 1400s Spanish scholar, writes that Moshe was called "man of God" here because he acted like God by forgiving the sins of the Jews and blessing them—as God does.

We know that classic commentators can have different opinions that can all be true. So let's say Moshe was both forgiving the people and defending them before he blessed them. What is it the commentators think that Moshe needed to forgive or defend? And why could Moshe not simply have been blessing the people before he died?

To understand this, we can wonder why might it have been difficult for Moshe to bless the people before he died. Well, the last verse in the previous Torah portion reads as follows: "And you [Moshe] will not go into the Land that I gave the children of Israel." Okay, we know that Moshe desperately desired to enter Israel, and we have various understandings of why Hashem did not allow Moshe into the Land. Back in *Parashat Va'etchanan*, Moshe was speaking to the Jewish People when he said, "Hashem was angry at me because of you, and He [Hashem] would not listen to me."[1] It seems that Moshe was blaming the people for Hashem's decision to forbid him to enter the Promised Land.

When we do not get what we want, it is certainly human to resent the people we think got in the way of our dreams. From the verse in *Parashat Va'etchanan*, it seems Moshe's human nature is on display. Yet Moshe, being Godly, does not leave it at that. In this *parashah*, Moshe shows that he has moved past his human nature, knowing that the end goal is not just to accept his fate, or even just to forgive the people, but to wholeheartedly bless the people.

With this awareness, we can understand why Moshe would want to be at the point of defending (i.e., explaining the behavior of) the people. For then he could know that he had fully forgiven the people and his blessing could be *b'lev shalem*—wholehearted.

I certainly do not claim to know through what process Moshe became a "man of God." I do, though, know that it is much more difficult to be a "man of God" amid people than alone. Moshe certainly was already Godly amid his flock of sheep in Midyan before Hashem pushed him to be the leader of the most stubborn people!

We can relate, because we know that our most difficult struggles on the road to being Godly involve other people. So we need a process, a plan, some kind of way to move to a place of wholeheartedly blessing someone whose actions and words have played a role in hurting us.

(Crucial caveat: The Jewish People were not purposely attempting to shut Moshe off from his dream of entering the Promised Land. They were simply displaying human selfishness, as most of us do, and their selfishness played a role in Moshe's fate. The following formula is for regular use regarding normal people in our lives. I do still believe the

---

1   *Devarim* 3:26.

Faith and Secure

SUKKOT

Why do we sit in the sukkah? The Talmud discusses two reasons, both of which are true. In the desert, after we left Egypt:

- Jews built huts in the desert.
- God's protective clouds surrounded the Jews in the desert.

If Judaism is about keeping the memory of an ancient heritage alive, then the festival is just a time of commemoration, and the information about the huts suffices. But we need some insight here because Judaism is an eternally applicable way of life. It is God's recipe for individual, national, and global fulfillment. I want to connect to the timeless message of those ancient huts and understand the purpose of those desert clouds.

The Jews built temporary homes under circumstances of undeniable recognition that everything in their possession was from and for Hashem. Although we may not live with the same absolute faith, it is certainly honorable to strive to build our homes with that understanding. We do not live without homes and possessions. We don't pretend

So I wondered where to hang the *Mizrach* painting. In this world, it makes sense to hang a sign that says "East" on an east-facing wall. However:

- If I hang it on the eastern wall of my home, it will indicate direction and lose its meaning.
- If I hang it on the northern wall, facing Israel, I am aligning the picture with its meaning, yet misleading the direction seekers of "this world" direction.

Still, "this world" directions are temporary. Rabbeinu Bachya, great scholar of the mid 1300s, tells us that our ancestors knew that the sukkot were reminders that all dwellings would be temporary on the road to the Land of Israel. Once in their own land, and even more so with the Beit Hamikdash, they would experience a sense of permanence. Our own sukkah is meant to remind us that all is temporary except the ultimate Infinite One.

The festival of Sukkot is called *Zeman Simchateinu*, "time of our happiness." About what are we happy? We are rejoicing in our vulnerability with the recognition that we are in God's hands, and He is the only true permanence.

Years ago, our four-year-old son reassured us, "In the sukkah, Hashem protects us from the elephants." Clearly, he was confusing elephants with elements. A statement that seemed absolutely incorrect at the time and place, however, seemed somewhat correct later on when we lived in South Africa.

In other words, on some days he might be right, which can sometimes be left. While east can sometimes be north.